Chicken with Prosciutto and Tomatoes
over Polenta, page 72

Cooking Light®

Chicken

Oxmoor
House®

ISBN: 0-8487-3063-1
Library of Congress Control Number:
2006921189
Printed in the United States of America
Fourth printing 2006

Be sure to check with your health-care provider
before making any changes in your diet.

Oxmoor House, Inc.
Editor in Chief: Nancy Fitzpatrick Wyatt
Executive Editor: Katherine M. Eakin
Copy Chief: Allison Long Lowery

Cooking Light® Chicken
Editor: Heather Averett
Food Editors: Anne Cain, M.S., R.D.;
    Alyson Moreland Haynes
Copy Editor: Diane Rose
Editorial Assistants: Julie Boston,
    Brigette Gaucher
Photography Director: Jim Bathie
Senior Photo Stylist: Kay E. Clarke
Photo Stylist: Katherine Eckert
Director, Test Kitchens: Elizabeth Tyler Austin
Assistant Director, Test Kitchens:
    Julie Christopher
Test Kitchens Staff: Kristi Carter,
    Nicole Lee Faber, Kathleen Royal Phillips,
    Elise Weis, Kelley Self Wilton
Director of Production: Laura Lockhart
Publishing Systems Administrator: Rick Tucker
Production Manager: Greg A. Amason
Production Assistant: Faye Porter Bonner

Contributors:
Designer: Carol Damsky
Indexer: Mary Ann Laurens
Editorial Interns: Rachel Quinlivan, R.D.;
    Mary Catherine Shamblin;
    Vanessa Rusch Thomas; Ashley Wells
Photographers: Beau Gustafson, Lee Harrelson
Photo Stylist: Lydia DeGaris-Pursell

To order additional publications, call
1-800-765-6400, or visit oxmoorhouse.com

CONTENTS

Essential Chicken   8

The basics. The classics. The very best
gotta-have recipes. From roasted
chicken to potpie, these are the chicken
recipes that no *Cooking Light* cook should
ever be without.

Jump-Start Meals   30

Looking for solutions to get you in and
out of the kitchen in no time? For
salads, soup, sandwiches, and more, turn
to these practical and proven recipes
that start with rotisserie chicken or
precooked chicken from the deli.

Dinner Tonight   52

From tacos to tender cuts dressed in
simple, mouthwatering sauces, here are
our staff's quick, easy answers to that
everyday question "What's for dinner?"

One-Dish Meals   74

These hearty meals help you get family-pleasing food on the table fast and save you clean-up hassle.

On the Grill   96

Fire it up! For summer or winter, here are great grilling recipes for fresh tastes and fun family times. From an Indonesian saté to an all-American barbecue, there's a world of lively flavor in this inherently healthy technique.

Casual Entertaining 116

Dress it up or dress it down. These great-looking, great-tasting dishes—from a classy chicken marsala to an exotic Oaxacan specialty—are impressive enough for guests but surprisingly simple to prepare. From fancy to family-friendly, these no-fail recipes are great for company any day of the week.

Cooking Light®
Editor in Chief: Mary Kay Culpepper
Executive Editor: Billy R. Sims
Art Director: Susan Waldrip Dendy
Managing Editor: Maelynn Cheung
Senior Food Editor: Alison Mann Ashton
Senior Editor: Anamary Pelayo
Features Editor: Phillip Rhodes
Projects Editor: Mary Simpson Creel, M.S., R.D.
Associate Food Editors: Timothy Q. Cebula,
    Ann Taylor Pittman
Assistant Food Editor: Kathy C. Kitchens, R.D.
Assistant Editor: Cindy Hatcher
Contributing Beauty Editor: Carol Straley
Test Kitchens Director: Vanessa Taylor Johnson
Food Stylist: Kellie Gerber Kelley
Assistant Food Stylist: M. Kathleen Kanen
Test Kitchens Professionals: Sam Brannock,
    Kathryn Conrad, Mary H. Drennen,
    Jan Jacks Moon, Tiffany Vickers,
    Mike Wilson
Assistant Art Director: Maya Metz Logue
Senior Designers: Fernande Bondarenko,
    J. Shay McNamee
Designer: Brigette Mayer
Senior Photographers: Becky Luigart-Stayner,
    Randy Mayor
Senior Photo Stylist: Cindy Barr
Photo Stylists: Melanie J. Clarke, Jan Gautro
Digital Photo Stylist: Jan A. Smith
Studio Assistant: Celine Chenoweth
Copy Chief: Maria Parker Hopkins
Senior Copy Editor: Susan Roberts
Copy Editor: Johannah Paiva
Production Manager: Liz Rhoades
Production Editors: Joanne McCrary Brasseal,
    Hazel R. Eddins
Administrative Coordinator: Carol D. Johnson
Office Manager: Rita K. Jackson
Editorial Assistants: Melissa Hoover,
    Brandy Rushing
Correspondence Editor: Michelle Gibson Daniels
Interns: Rachel Cardina, Marie Hegler,
    Emily Self

CookingLight.com
Editor: Jennifer Middleton Richards
Online Producer: Abigail Masters

Cover: *Chicken with Green Olives* (page 70)

Welcome

Chicken is versatile, dependable, and utterly enjoyable. But there's another thing that chicken is, and that's essential. For a *Cooking Light*® cook, chicken is a favorite food, served often and happily.

In this cookbook, you'll find the chicken recipes we believe to be the essential recipes for every *Cooking Light* cook. These recipes are our tried-and-true classics—ones we love to make again and again.

Each chapter offers mouthwatering, flavorful recipes, complete with nutritional analyses that will help you to eat smart, be fit, and live well.

So whether you're looking for a down-home recipe for Old-Fashioned Chicken Potpie or for something a little more upscale, such as Chicken Marsala, you're sure to find it in this edition of *The Cooking Light Cook's Essential Recipe Collection.*

Very truly yours,

Mary Kay Culpepper
Editor in Chief

essential
chicken

Sunday Roasted Chicken with Giblet Gravy

When roasting chicken, a thermometer is essential. And you have a choice between three types—standard, instant read, and digital. The standard meat thermometer is inserted into the meaty part of the thigh and remains in place until the chicken is done. The instant-read thermometer is inserted into the thigh, read, and then taken out. You have to check the temperature early and frequently to avoid overcooking. The digital thermometer (our favorite) has a display unit that sits outside the oven so you can keep track of the temperature without opening the oven door.

1 (6-pound) roasting chicken
2 (14-ounce) cans fat-free, less-sodium chicken broth, divided
1 carrot, cut into 2-inch pieces
1 celery stalk, cut into 2-inch pieces
1 onion, quartered
2 large garlic cloves, unpeeled and halved
2 bay leaves
1 teaspoon kosher salt
1 tablespoon dried thyme
1 tablespoon dried rubbed sage
¼ cup all-purpose flour
¼ teaspoon black pepper

1. Remove giblets and neck from chicken, discarding liver. Cut off wing tips, and combine with giblets, neck, 3 cups broth, carrot, celery, onion, garlic, and bay leaves in a saucepan. Bring to a boil; partially cover, reduce heat, and simmer 45 minutes. Strain broth mixture through a sieve into a bowl, reserving broth and giblets. Mince giblets; add to strained broth, and set aside. Discard remaining solids.

2. Preheat oven to 375°.

3. Rinse chicken with cold water, and pat dry. Trim excess fat. Starting at neck cavity, loosen skin from breast and drumsticks by inserting fingers, gently pushing between skin and meat. Combine salt, thyme, and sage in a small bowl. Rub thyme mixture under loosened skin and over breast and drumsticks. Gently press skin to secure. Tie legs with string.

4. Place chicken, breast side up, on rack of a broiler pan or roasting pan. Insert a meat thermometer into meaty part of thigh, making sure not to touch bone. Bake at 375° for 1 hour and 30 minutes or until thermometer registers 180° and juices run clear. Cover chicken loosely with foil; let stand 10 minutes for chicken to reabsorb juices. Discard skin. Remove rack from pan. Add ½ cup broth to drippings in pan, scraping pan to loosen browned bits. Place a zip-top plastic bag inside a 2-cup measure. Pour drippings into bag; let stand 10 minutes (fat will rise to the top). Seal bag; carefully snip off 1 corner of bag; drain liquid into saucepan, stopping before fat layer reaches opening. Discard fat.

5. Add reserved giblet mixture to broth mixture in saucepan.

6. Combine remaining ½ cup broth and flour in a bowl. Add flour mixture to saucepan; bring to a boil. Reduce heat; cook 10 minutes, stirring constantly. Stir in pepper. Serve with chicken. Yield: 8 servings (serving size: 4 ounces chicken and ⅓ cup gravy).

CALORIES 217 (20% from fat); FAT 4.8g (sat 1.2g, mono 1.5g, poly 1.2g); PROTEIN 37.3g; CARB 4.1g; FIBER 1g; CHOL 113mg; IRON 2.4mg; SODIUM 651mg; CALC 29mg

Grilled Split Chicken with Rosemary and Garlic

1 (4-pound) broiler-fryer
  chicken
½ cup low-fat buttermilk
1 tablespoon chopped fresh
  rosemary
¾ teaspoon salt
½ teaspoon hot pepper sauce
  (such as Tabasco)
2 garlic cloves, minced
2 cups water
Cooking spray

For direct grilling, you place food on a grill rack directly over hot coals. But there's also indirect grilling, which is similar to oven-roasting; it's ideal for large foods such as whole chickens, turkey breasts, and roasts that need a longer cooking time. Both sides of the grill are fired up; then one side is turned off. A disposable aluminum foil pan (drip pan) containing water (or wine, broth, or another liquid) is placed over the coals on the side of the grill where the heat has been turned off. The food is placed on the rack over the pan.

1. Remove and discard giblets and neck from chicken. Rinse chicken with cold water; pat dry. Trim excess fat. Place chicken, breast side down, on a cutting surface. Cut chicken in half lengthwise along backbone, cutting to, but not through, other side (do not cut through breastbone). Turn chicken over. Starting at neck cavity, loosen skin from breast and drumsticks by inserting fingers, gently pushing between skin and meat. Place chicken, breast side up, in a large, shallow dish. Combine buttermilk and next 4 ingredients; pour under skin and over surface of chicken. Lift wing tips up and over back; tuck under chicken. Cover and marinate in refrigerator 24 hours.

2. To prepare for indirect grilling on a gas grill, preheat grill to medium-hot using both burners. After preheating, turn left burner off (leave right burner on). Place a disposable aluminum foil pan on briquettes on left side. Pour 2 cups water in pan. Place chicken on grill rack coated with cooking spray. Place chicken, skin side down, on grill rack covering left burner. Discard marinade. Cover and grill 2 hours or until a thermometer registers 180°, turning halfway through cooking time. Discard skin before serving. Yield: 5 servings (serving size: 4 ounces).

Note: To prepare for indirect grilling on a charcoal grill, place a disposable aluminum foil pan in bottom of grill; pour water in pan. Arrange charcoal around pan; prepare charcoal fire, and let burn 15 to 20 minutes. Coat grill rack with cooking spray; place rack on grill. Place chicken on grill rack over foil pan, and proceed with method as directed above.

CALORIES 218 (21% from fat); FAT 5.2g (sat 1.4g, mono 1.6g, poly 1.3g); PROTEIN 38.5g; CARB 1.7g; FIBER 0.1g; CHOL 121mg; IRON 2mg; SODIUM 526mg; CALC 51mg

Oven-Fried Chicken Fingers with Honey-Mustard Dipping Sauce

A combination of dry bread-crumbs and crushed cornflakes produces the crispiest, most flavorful crust on oven-fried chicken. The easiest way to coat chicken with a breading mixture is to use a zip-top plastic bag. Place the breading mixture in the bag, and add the chicken a few pieces at a time. Close the top of the bag, and shake well.

Sauce:
¼ cup honey
¼ cup spicy brown mustard

Chicken:
1½ pounds chicken breast
    tenders (about 16 pieces)
1 cup low-fat buttermilk
1 cup coarsely crushed
    cornflakes
½ cup seasoned breadcrumbs
2 tablespoons instant minced
    onion
2 teaspoons paprika
½ teaspoon dried thyme
½ teaspoon black pepper
1 tablespoon canola oil

1. To prepare sauce, combine honey and mustard in a small bowl; cover and chill.

2. To prepare chicken, combine chicken and buttermilk in a shallow dish; cover and chill 15 minutes. Drain chicken, discarding liquid.

3. Preheat oven to 400°.

4. Combine cornflakes and next 5 ingredients in a large zip-top plastic bag; add 4 chicken pieces to bag. Seal and shake to coat. Repeat procedure with remaining chicken. Spread oil evenly on a jelly-roll pan; arrange chicken in a single layer on pan. Bake at 400° for 5 minutes on each side or until done. Serve with sauce. Yield: 4 servings (serving size: 4 chicken tenders and 1 tablespoon sauce).

CALORIES 231 (13% from fat); FAT 3.4g (sat 0.6g, mono 1.4g, poly 1g); PROTEIN 22.6g; CARB 26g; FIBER 1.7g; CHOL 50mg; IRON 3.2mg; SODIUM 393mg; CALC 44mg

These chicken fingers will have all of your loved ones—especially kids—begging for an encore! The crunchy coating of the lightly breaded chicken and the sweet and slightly tangy zing of the dipping sauce are a perfect pairing. With this recipe in your repertoire, you'll spend less time at the drive-through and keep your family healthier, too.

Thai-Style Stir-Fried Chicken

Stir-frying is a low-fat technique that works well with a variety of foods, including chicken. Instead of a wok, we prefer using a stir-fry pan with a nonreactive stainless-steel or anodized-aluminum surface. Unlike a round-bottom wok, which requires a ring on which the vessel can sit, a stir-fry pan has a wide, flat bottom that rests evenly on a smooth-top cooking surface, either gas or electric. A stir-fry pan typically has a long stay-cool handle and a small helper handle on the opposite end. While the pan is available in 8- to 14-inch diameters, we like the 12-inch model the best—it doesn't require too much storage space, yet it provides more than enough cooking surface.

¼ cup rice vinegar
2 tablespoons brown sugar
2 tablespoons fresh lime juice
2 teaspoons red curry paste
⅛ teaspoon crushed red pepper
1 pound skinless, boneless chicken breast, cut into bite-sized pieces
1½ tablespoons vegetable oil, divided
1 cup chopped onion
1 cup chopped carrot
1 (8-ounce) package presliced mushrooms
½ cup light coconut milk
1 tablespoon fish sauce
½ teaspoon salt
1 cup fresh bean sprouts
¼ cup chopped fresh cilantro

1. Combine first 5 ingredients in a large zip-top plastic bag. Add chicken; seal and marinate in refrigerator 30 minutes, turning once.
2. Remove chicken from bag, reserving marinade. Heat 1 tablespoon oil in a large nonstick skillet or stir-fry pan over medium-high heat. Add chicken, and stir-fry 4 minutes. Remove chicken from pan; keep warm. Add remaining 1½ teaspoons oil to pan. Add onion and carrot; stir-fry 2 minutes. Add mushrooms; stir-fry 3 minutes. Add reserved marinade, scraping pan to loosen browned bits. Add coconut milk and fish sauce; bring to a boil. Reduce heat, and simmer 1 minute. Stir in chicken and salt; cook 1 minute. Top with sprouts and cilantro. Yield: 4 servings (serving size: 1 cup chicken mixture, ¼ cup sprouts, and 1 tablespoon cilantro).

CALORIES 271 (28% from fat); FAT 8.4g (sat 2.2g, mono 1.6g, poly 3.4g); PROTEIN 29.7g; CARB 19.6g; FIBER 2.9g; CHOL 66mg; IRON 2.2mg; SODIUM 767mg; CALC 43mg

Once the chicken and vegetables are prepped, the cooking goes quickly. Have all of the ingredients close at hand to whip up this sweet-hot dinner on a busy evening. It will be a beautiful Thai-inspired presentation that you and your dinner guests won't soon forget.

Broiled Chicken Breasts with Vegetable Sauté

Broiling is a low-fat cooking method that is particularly good for relatively small, tender cuts of meat. When you broil, the food is placed on a broiler pan (usually on the top rack of the oven), and the heat source is above the food. Generally, you need to turn the meat about halfway through the cooking time to get both sides of the meat evenly browned. Like grilling, broiling is a low-fat cooking method because some of the fat cooks out of the meat into the pan.

1 teaspoon garlic powder
½ teaspoon salt, divided
¼ teaspoon black pepper, divided
4 (6-ounce) skinless, boneless chicken breast halves
Cooking spray
1 tablespoon olive oil
1 (8-ounce) package presliced mushrooms
1 small zucchini, quartered lengthwise and sliced (about 5 ounces)
4 garlic cloves, minced
1 cup chopped plum tomato
½ cup chopped red onion
½ cup chopped fresh basil
4 teaspoons balsamic vinegar
¼ cup (1 ounce) grated fresh Parmesan cheese

1. Preheat broiler.
2. Combine garlic powder, ¼ teaspoon salt, and ⅛ teaspoon pepper in a small bowl; sprinkle chicken with garlic powder mixture. Place chicken on a broiler pan coated with cooking spray, and broil 6 minutes on each side or until done. Remove chicken from pan; keep warm.
3. Heat olive oil in a large nonstick skillet over medium-high heat. Add remaining ¼ teaspoon salt, mushrooms, zucchini, and minced garlic; sauté 2 minutes. Add remaining ⅛ teaspoon pepper, tomato, onion, basil, and vinegar; sauté 3 minutes. Serve vegetable mixture over chicken; sprinkle with cheese. Yield: 4 servings (serving size: 1 chicken breast half, ½ cup vegetables, and 1 tablespoon cheese).

CALORIES 284 (23% from fat); FAT 7.3g (sat 2g, mono 3.5g, poly 1.1g); PROTEIN 44.4g; CARB 9.4g; FIBER 2.2g; CHOL 103mg; IRON 2.2mg; SODIUM 488mg; CALC 106mg

If your idea of the perfect chicken dish is one that looks and tastes impressive but is simple to prepare and cook, then this recipe is a keeper. It's a terrific entrée to serve any night of the week or for a weekend dinner party. It serves up beautifully—and colorfully—alongside a simple salad and crusty French bread.

Sautéed Chicken Breasts with Sherry-Vinegar Sauce

4 (6-ounce) skinless, boneless chicken breast halves
½ teaspoon salt
¼ teaspoon black pepper
1 teaspoon butter
1 teaspoon olive oil
½ cup minced shallots
¾ cup fat-free, less-sodium chicken broth
3 tablespoons sherry vinegar
2 tablespoons whipping cream
1 tablespoon chopped fresh parsley

1. Sprinkle chicken with salt and pepper. Heat butter and oil in a large nonstick skillet over medium-high heat. Add chicken; cook 4 minutes on each side or until done. Remove from pan; keep warm. Add shallots to pan; sauté 1 minute. Stir in chicken broth and vinegar, and cook 4 minutes or until liquid is reduced by half. Add whipping cream; cook 1 minute. Serve sauce with chicken. Sprinkle with parsley. Yield: 4 servings (serving size: 1 chicken breast half and 1 tablespoon sauce).

CALORIES 194 (29% from fat); FAT 6.3g (sat 2.9g, mono 2.2g, poly 0.6g); PROTEIN 27.4g; CARB 5.6g; FIBER 0.4g; CHOL 78mg; IRON 1.3mg; SODIUM 457mg; CALC 33mg

Nonstick skillets are a staple in the *Cooking Light* Test Kitchens. They are generally used for quick sautéing and for stir-frying meats, seafood, and vegetables. While nonstick coatings are durable, you can prolong their life by not overheating them, especially when they are empty. These pans' coatings are made of fluoropolymer substances that are damaged by excess heat, so stay away from the high setting on the cooktop dial. Also, if the recipe calls for cooking spray, coat the pan after it has heated.

Simple and luscious, this dish comes together in a hurry and requires only one pan. Serving the pan-sautéed chicken with lumpy, rustic mashed potatoes and steamed green beans makes for a classic dinner combination.

Chicken Scallopini

To easily pound a chicken breast, place each breast between two sheets of heavy-duty plastic wrap; pound to desired thickness—usually ¼- to ½-inch thick—using a meat mallet or rolling pin.

4 (6-ounce) skinless, boneless chicken breast halves
2 teaspoons fresh lemon juice
¼ teaspoon salt
¼ teaspoon black pepper
⅓ cup Italian-seasoned breadcrumbs
Cooking spray
½ cup fat-free, less-sodium chicken broth
¼ cup dry white wine
4 teaspoons capers
1 tablespoon butter
Flat-leaf parsley (optional)

1. Place each chicken breast half between 2 sheets of heavy-duty plastic wrap, and pound to ¼-inch thickness using a meat mallet or rolling pin. Brush chicken with lemon juice, and sprinkle with salt and pepper. Dredge chicken in breadcrumbs.

2. Heat a large nonstick skillet over medium-high heat. Coat pan with cooking spray. Add chicken to pan; cook 3 minutes on each side or until done. Remove from pan; keep warm.

3. Add broth and wine to pan; cook 30 seconds, stirring constantly. Remove from heat. Stir in capers and butter. Garnish with parsley, if desired. Yield: 4 servings (serving size: 1 chicken breast half and 1 tablespoon sauce).

CALORIES 206 (20% from fat); FAT 4.6g (sat 2.2g, mono 1.3g, poly 0.5g); PROTEIN 29.2g; CARB 7.7g; FIBER 0.6g; CHOL 76mg; IRON 1.6mg; SODIUM 657mg; CALC 27mg

Pounding the chicken breast halves cuts the cooking time in half while leaving the chicken moist and tender. Orzo sautéed with zucchini and cherry tomatoes makes a great side dish, but you may also substitute rice in place of the orzo.

Chicken Breasts Stuffed with Artichokes, Lemon, and Goat Cheese

Browning meats is a technique used to help develop an appealing color and seal in flavor and juices. To brown chicken, make sure your skillet is hot enough to make an immediate sizzle when you add the food. Be sure not to crowd the food in the pan; otherwise, the food will steam rather than brown. Don't move the food around or turn it too often. Just leave it to sizzle until it becomes a nice golden brown color, and then turn it.

2½ tablespoons Italian-
    seasoned breadcrumbs
 2 teaspoons grated lemon rind
 ¼ teaspoon salt
 ¼ teaspoon freshly ground
    black pepper
 1 (6-ounce) jar marinated
    artichoke hearts, drained
    and chopped
 1 (3-ounce) package herbed
    goat cheese, softened
 4 (6-ounce) skinless, boneless
    chicken breast halves
Cooking spray

1. Preheat oven to 375°.
2. Combine first 6 ingredients; stir well.
3. Place each chicken breast half between 2 sheets of heavy-duty plastic wrap; pound to ¼-inch thickness using a meat mallet or rolling pin. Top each breast half with 2 tablespoons cheese mixture; roll up jelly-roll fashion; secure each roll with wooden picks.
4. Heat a large nonstick skillet over medium-high heat. Coat pan with cooking spray. Add chicken to pan; cook 3 minutes on each side or until browned. Wrap handle of pan with foil; bake at 375° for 15 minutes or until done. Yield: 4 servings (serving size: 1 chicken breast half).

CALORIES 234 (30% from fat); FAT 7.8g (sat 3.5g, mono 1.4g, poly 0.5g); PROTEIN 33g; CARB 7.2g; FIBER 1.5g; CHOL 78mg; IRON 1.6mg; SODIUM 545mg; CALC 49mg

Browning the chicken on the stovetop and finishing it in the oven frees you up to put the final touches on your side dishes—such as a fluffy rice pilaf and tender spinach leaves. You can stuff the chicken breasts and chill them up to four hours before serving. If you want to impress guests, this recipe is perfect for you.

Quick Coq au Vin

A good rule of thumb when cooking with wine is to use a wine that is the same or has similar qualities to the wine you'll serve with the meal. For this traditional French dish, a dry red wine works well, particularly a Burgundy or pinot noir.

¼ cup all-purpose flour
1 teaspoon dried thyme
½ teaspoon salt
6 (6-ounce) skinless, boneless chicken thighs
1 tablespoon olive oil
6 cups quartered cremini mushrooms
2 cups (¼-inch-thick) slices carrot
⅓ cup (¼-inch-thick) slices Canadian bacon
1 cup dry red wine
1 cup fat-free, less-sodium chicken broth
1 tablespoon tomato paste
Thyme sprigs (optional)

1. Combine flour, thyme, and salt in a zip-top plastic bag; add chicken. Seal and shake to coat. Remove chicken from bag, shaking off excess flour mixture.

2. Heat oil in a large nonstick skillet over medium-high heat. Add chicken; cook 8 minutes or until browned, turning frequently. Remove chicken from pan.

3. Add cremini mushrooms, carrot, and bacon to pan; sauté 2 minutes. Stir in wine, chicken broth, and tomato paste, and cook 9 minutes. Return chicken to pan; cook 8 minutes or until chicken is done. Garnish with thyme, if desired. Yield: 6 servings (serving size: about 1¼ cups).

CALORIES 293 (30% from fat); FAT 9.7g (sat 2.2g, mono 4g, poly 2g); PROTEIN 38.3g; CARB 12.4g; FIBER 2g; CHOL 145mg; IRON 2.8mg; SODIUM 579mg; CALC 50mg

This quick take on the classic long-simmered French dish is composed of succulent chicken, meaty mushrooms, salty bacon, and herbs—all cooked in dry red wine. Cooking uncovered over medium-high heat reduces the liquid and concentrates its flavors in a fraction of the time required for the traditional dish.

Old-Fashioned Chicken Potpie

Chicken broth, available in cans or cartons, is a staple ingredient in a well-stocked pantry. Use it as the foundation for soups, sauces, or this chicken potpie, and you'll have a dish ready in just minutes. Be sure to read the nutrition label, as the sodium and fat contents vary among brands.

Crust:
   1 cup all-purpose flour
   3 tablespoons ice water
   1 teaspoon cider vinegar
   ¼ teaspoon salt
   ¼ cup vegetable shortening

Filling:
   3 cups fat-free, less-sodium chicken broth, divided
   2⅓ cups cubed red potato (about 1 pound)
   1 cup (¼-inch-thick) slices carrot
   2 teaspoons butter
   ½ cup chopped shallots or onion
   ½ cup all-purpose flour
   1 cup frozen petite green peas
   ¾ teaspoon salt
   ¼ teaspoon dried thyme
Dash of black pepper
   2 cups diced cooked chicken

Remaining Ingredients:
Cooking spray
   2 teaspoons 1% low-fat milk

1. To prepare crust, lightly spoon 1 cup flour into a dry measuring cup, and level with a knife. Combine ¼ cup flour, ice water, and vinegar in a small bowl. Combine ¾ cup flour and ¼ teaspoon salt in a large bowl; cut in shortening with a pastry blender or 2 knives until mixture resembles coarse meal. Add vinegar mixture; stir just until moist. Gently press mixture into a 5-inch circle on heavy-duty plastic wrap; cover with additional plastic wrap. Chill 15 minutes. Roll dough, still covered, into a 10-inch circle. Place dough in refrigerator.

2. Preheat oven to 400°.

3. To prepare filling, bring 2½ cups broth to a boil in a medium saucepan. Add potato and carrot; cook 10 minutes. Drain mixture in a colander over a bowl, reserving cooking liquid.

4. Melt butter in a large nonstick skillet over medium heat. Add shallots; cook 3 minutes. Lightly spoon ½ cup flour into a dry measuring cup; level with a knife. Combine ½ cup flour and remaining ½ cup broth, and stir with a whisk. Add to skillet. Stir in potato mixture, reserved cooking liquid, peas, ¾ teaspoon salt, thyme, and pepper. Cook 10 minutes until thickened; stir in chicken. Remove from heat, and cool slightly. Spoon chicken mixture into a 10-inch deep-dish pie plate coated with cooking spray. Remove 1 sheet of plastic wrap from dough. Place dough on top of chicken mixture, pressing to edge of dish. Remove top sheet of plastic wrap. Cut 5 slits in top of crust to allow steam to escape. Gently brush crust with milk. Bake at 400° for 45 minutes or until golden. Let stand 10 minutes. Yield: 6 servings (servings size: about 1 cup).

CALORIES 362 (29% from fat); FAT 11.5g (sat 4.5g, mono 3g, poly 2.9g); PROTEIN 22.1g; CARB 41.3g; FIBER 3.6g; CHOL 43mg; IRON 3mg; SODIUM 764mg; CALC 38mg

jump-start meals

Curried Chicken Salad

Indigenous to India, authentic curry powder is a mixture of pungent spices that come in varying degrees of heat—mild, medium, or hot. It may contain over 20 spices, including cardamom, cloves, cumin, fennel seed, and red and black pepper. The longer the list of ingredients, the more complex the flavor.

1½ cups chopped cooked chicken breast (about 8 ounces)
½ cup halved seedless red grapes
½ cup diced peeled apple
2 tablespoons diced pineapple
1 tablespoon dried currants
3 tablespoons low-fat mayonnaise
1 teaspoon honey
½ teaspoon curry powder
½ teaspoon fresh lemon juice
⅛ teaspoon salt
⅛ teaspoon freshly ground black pepper
1 tablespoon sliced almonds, toasted

1. Combine first 5 ingredients in a large bowl. Combine mayonnaise and next 5 ingredients, stirring with a whisk. Pour mayonnaise mixture over chicken mixture, and toss gently to coat. Sprinkle with almonds. Cover and chill. Yield: 2 servings (serving size: 1¼ cups).

CALORIES 303 (21% from fat); FAT 7.2g (sat 1.3g, mono 2.3g, poly 1.3g); PROTEIN 33.8g; CARB 25.7g; FIBER 1.9g; CHOL 89mg; IRON 1.7mg; SODIUM 435mg; CALC 37mg

This recipe is easy to make, and if you use rotisserie chicken, you can have it ready even faster. For a light dinner, serve with hot crusty bread or rolls. And if you're not too shy with curry, add some more for a stronger, spicier taste. Double the recipe for a sure crowd-pleaser. If you're hosting a casual luncheon or picnic, add this flavorful recipe to the menu.

Smoky Bacon and Blue Cheese Chicken Salad Pitas

Also called pocket bread, this Middle Eastern flatbread can be made of white or whole wheat flour. Each pita round is split horizontally to form a pocket. Throughout the Middle East, pitas are served with meals or cut into wedges and used as dippers for dishes such as baba ghanoush and hummus.

¾ cup plain fat-free yogurt
¼ cup (1 ounce) crumbled blue cheese
2 tablespoons light mayonnaise
½ teaspoon freshly ground black pepper
3 cups shredded romaine lettuce
1½ cups shredded cooked chicken breast (about 6 ounces)
4 bacon slices, cooked and crumbled
2 medium tomatoes, seeded and chopped
4 (6-inch) whole wheat pitas, cut in half

1. Combine first 4 ingredients, stirring well. Combine lettuce, chicken, bacon, and tomatoes in a medium bowl, stirring well. Drizzle yogurt mixture over chicken mixture; toss gently to coat. Spoon ½ cup chicken salad into each pita half. Serve immediately. Yield: 4 servings (serving size: 2 stuffed pita halves).

CALORIES 375 (29% from fat); FAT 12.1g (sat 3.7g, mono 3.6g, poly 3.1g); PROTEIN 26.1g; CARB 43.8g; FIBER 6.3g; CHOL 55mg; IRON 3.5mg; SODIUM 696mg; CALC 130mg

The BLT sandwich is the inspiration for this tangy salad. You can make the chicken salad ahead and place it in pita halves just before serving. These pitas are a wonderful way to take advantage of juicy, ruby-red vine-ripened tomatoes.

Chicken and Brie Sandwich with Roasted Cherry Tomatoes

Brie is characterized by an edible white rind and a cream-colored, buttery-soft interior that should "ooze" when the cheese is at the peak of ripeness. Brie can be made from raw or pasteurized whole or skim milk. To select Brie at its peak, choose one that is plump and resilient to the touch. Its rind should show some pale brown edges.

1 teaspoon olive oil
2 cups halved cherry tomatoes (about 1 pound)
2 tablespoons balsamic vinegar
1 tablespoon chopped fresh thyme
¼ teaspoon kosher salt
⅛ teaspoon black pepper
¼ cup low-fat mayonnaise
1 tablespoon whole-grain Dijon mustard
1 garlic clove, minced
1 (16-ounce) loaf French bread, cut in half horizontally
3 ounces Brie cheese, sliced
3 cups shredded cooked chicken breast (about 1 pound)
2 teaspoons extravirgin olive oil
1 teaspoon balsamic vinegar
⅛ teaspoon kosher salt
2 cups fresh spinach

1. Preheat oven to 300°.
2. Heat 1 teaspoon olive oil in a large nonstick skillet over medium-high heat. Add tomatoes; cook 4 minutes, stirring once. Remove from heat; stir in 2 tablespoons vinegar. Sprinkle tomatoes with thyme, ¼ teaspoon salt, and pepper. Wrap handle of pan with foil; bake at 300° for 15 minutes. Keep warm.
3. Combine mayonnaise, mustard, and garlic in a small bowl. Spread mayonnaise mixture evenly over top half of bread loaf. Spoon tomatoes evenly over bottom half of loaf. Arrange Brie over tomatoes; top with chicken. Combine 2 teaspoons oil, 1 teaspoon vinegar, and ⅛ teaspoon salt in a medium bowl, stirring with a whisk. Add spinach, tossing gently to coat. Top chicken with spinach mixture; replace top half of bread. Cut loaf into 6 pieces. Yield: 6 servings.

CALORIES 440 (25% from fat); FAT 12.3g (sat 4.2g, mono 4.9g, poly 1.9g); PROTEIN 34.3g; CARB 46.7g; FIBER 3.9g; CHOL 78mg; IRON 3.7mg; SODIUM 826mg; CALC 119mg

This chicken sandwich bursts with delicious flavors! Remember that a good balsamic vinegar makes all the difference in the roasted tomatoes. If time is of the essence, replace the shredded cooked chicken breast with Tyson grilled chicken strips or canned chicken breast. Turkey will also make a good stand-in.

Cuban Chicken Pizza

Although small, cumin seeds pack a punch when added to a recipe. They have a nutty, peppery flavor, and they are oblong in shape, longitudinally ridged, and yellow-brown in color. These seeds are an essential component of curry powders and chile powders, and they play a major role in Latin American, Indian, and Middle Eastern cuisines. They should be kept in a tightly sealed glass container in a cool, dark, dry place. Whole seeds will stay fresh for about one year. Toasting the seeds helps bring out their flavor.

4 (8-inch) fat-free flour tortillas
Cooking spray
1 (11-ounce) can no salt–added whole-kernel corn, drained
½ teaspoon cumin seeds
2 cups diced roasted chicken breast
1 (15-ounce) can black beans, rinsed and drained
1 garlic clove, minced
2 tablespoons fresh lime juice
¾ cup (3 ounces) shredded Monterey Jack cheese with jalapeño peppers
4 teaspoons chopped fresh cilantro

1. Preheat oven to 350°.
2. Place flour tortillas on a baking sheet coated with cooking spray. Bake at 350° for 10 minutes or until edges are light brown. Remove from oven; stack and press down to flatten. Set aside.
3. Heat a large nonstick skillet over medium-high heat; coat pan with cooking spray. Add corn to pan, and cook 1 minute or until lightly charred. Add cumin seeds; cook 5 seconds, stirring constantly. Add chicken, black beans, and garlic; cook 2 minutes or until thoroughly heated. Remove from heat; stir in lime juice.
4. Place tortillas on baking sheet. Spoon ¾ cup bean mixture onto each tortilla; top each with 3 tablespoons cheese. Bake at 350° for 2 minutes or until cheese melts. Sprinkle each pizza with 1 teaspoon cilantro. Yield: 4 servings (serving size: 1 pizza).

CALORIES 460 (20% from fat); FAT 10.2g (sat 4.8g, mono 2.9g, poly 1.7g); PROTEIN 37.7g; CARB 54.3g; FIBER 8.4g; CHOL 78mg; IRON 3.6mg; SODIUM 760mg; CALC 210mg

Bring a little of Havana to your home tonight. This dish receives five stars for convenience and taste! Toasting the corn in a skillet brings out its natural sweetness and adds a smoky note of flavor.

Chicken Quesadillas with Fruit Salsa and Avocado Cream

A papaya resembles a large pear and has pale green skin that gets yellow or orange blotches as it ripens. It has a hollow center with a mass of shiny black seeds. These seeds are edible and have a slightly peppery taste. Look for a papaya that gives a bit when pressed. The skin should be smooth and already starting to turn yellow. Store papayas at room temperature to allow them to ripen.

Cooking spray
1⅓ cups shredded carrot
1 cup thinly sliced green onions
1 cup (4 ounces) shredded Monterey Jack cheese with jalapeño peppers
8 (8-inch) fat-free flour tortillas
2 cups chopped ready-to-eat roasted skinless, boneless chicken breast (such as Tyson; about 2 breasts)
½ cup fresh cilantro leaves
Fruit Salsa
Avocado Cream
Cilantro sprigs (optional)

1. Heat a large nonstick skillet over medium-high heat. Coat pan with cooking spray. Add carrot and onions; sauté 5 minutes or until tender. Sprinkle 2 tablespoons cheese over each of 4 tortillas, and top evenly with carrot mixture. Top each tortilla with ½ cup chicken, 2 tablespoons cilantro, 2 tablespoons cheese, and a tortilla.

2. Heat pan over medium heat. Coat pan with cooking spray. Add 1 quesadilla, and cook 2 minutes on each side or until quesadilla is browned. Repeat with remaining quesadillas. Cut each quesadilla into 6 wedges. Arrange 4 quesadilla wedges on each of 6 plates. Top each serving with ⅔ cup Fruit Salsa, about 3 tablespoons Avocado Cream, and cilantro sprigs, if desired. Yield: 6 servings.

CALORIES 408 (28% from fat); FAT 12.5g (sat 4.9g, mono 5.4g, poly 1.2g); PROTEIN 20.6g; CARB 55.8g; FIBER 5.6g; CHOL 38mg; IRON 2.2mg; SODIUM 888mg; CALC 218mg

Fruit Salsa

1. Combine 2 cups coarsely chopped peeled ripe papaya or mango, 1½ cups coarsely chopped peeled kiwifruit, ¾ cup fresh corn kernels, ½ cup chopped red onion, ½ cup minced fresh cilantro, 3 tablespoons fresh lime juice, 1 tablespoon minced seeded jalapeño pepper, and ¼ teaspoon salt in a small bowl; cover and chill. Yield: 4 cups.

Avocado Cream

1. Place 1 peeled medium avocado (pitted and cut into chunks), ½ cup fat-free sour cream, and 2 tablespoons fresh lime juice in a blender; process until smooth. Spoon puréed mixture into a small bowl; stir in 2 tablespoons minced fresh cilantro. Cover and chill. Yield: 1⅓ cups.

Creamed Chicken

½ cup all-purpose flour
2¼ cups whole milk
1 cup frozen green peas,
  thawed
2 teaspoons chopped fresh
  sage
1 teaspoon butter
1 (10-ounce) package roasted
  skinless, boneless chicken
  breast (such as Perdue Short
  Cuts), chopped
1 tablespoon fresh lemon juice
¼ teaspoon freshly ground
  black pepper
Sage sprigs (optional)

1. Lightly spoon flour into a dry measuring cup, and level with a knife. Combine flour and ½ cup milk in a large saucepan over medium heat, stirring with a whisk until smooth. Stir in 1¾ cups milk. Cook 4 minutes or until thick, stirring constantly with a whisk.

2. Stir in peas, sage, butter, and chicken. Cook 2 minutes or until thoroughly heated. Remove from heat; stir in juice and pepper. Garnish with sage sprigs, if desired. Yield: 4 servings (serving size: about ¾ cup).

CALORIES 232 (23% from fat); FAT 6g (sat 3.6g, mono 1.8g, poly 0.4g); PROTEIN 20.9g; CARB 25.4g; FIBER 2.1g; CHOL 53mg; IRON 2.2mg; SODIUM 1,001mg; CALC 164mg

Research leaves us no room to doubt that calcium has a number of health benefits and may play a role in weight loss. As the best source of calcium, milk provides these benefits, whether you're using it for drinking or cooking. The recipe determines which type of milk is used. Take Creamed Chicken, for example. Using whole milk gives the dish a creamy, rich flavor that can't be achieved with reduced-fat milk.

This recipe comes together in a flash, and the peas add a nice touch of color. If you can't find roasted skinless, boneless chicken breast, buy a whole roasted chicken, and substitute 2¼ cups chopped cooked breast meat. Add the leftover chicken to soup, pasta, or a salad later in the week.

Creamy Chicken and Mushroom Crêpes

The portobello mushroom, which can easily measure 6 inches in diameter, has an open, flat cap. The comparatively newly named and marketed baby portobello, also called cremini, is smaller and has a smoother texture and a milder flavor. When buying, select plump, whole mushrooms that have an earthy aroma. To store, remove wrapping, spread mushrooms in a basket or tray, cover with a towel, and refrigerate. Do not moisten or set objects on top. If very fresh, they may last five to six days.

1 teaspoon butter
1 cup vertically sliced onion
1 garlic clove, minced
3 cups thinly sliced baby portobello mushroom caps (about 6 ounces)
¾ teaspoon salt
¼ teaspoon freshly ground black pepper
½ cup dry white wine
¾ cup fat-free, less-sodium chicken broth
2 teaspoons chopped fresh thyme
¼ cup crème fraîche
2 cups shredded roasted skinless, boneless chicken breast
6 (9-inch) packaged French crêpes (such as Melissa's)
Thyme sprigs (optional)

1. Melt butter in a large nonstick skillet over medium-high heat. Add onion and garlic; sauté 2 minutes or until onion begins to brown. Add mushrooms, salt, and pepper; cook 3 minutes or until liquid evaporates and mushrooms are tender, stirring frequently. Add wine, and cook 3 minutes or until liquid almost evaporates, stirring frequently. Add broth and chopped thyme; cook 2 minutes. Remove from heat; add crème fraîche, stirring until well blended. Add chicken, tossing to coat.

2. Place 1 crêpe on each of 6 plates. Spoon about ⅓ cup mushroom mixture into center of each crêpe; roll up. Garnish with thyme sprigs, if desired. Serve immediately. Yield: 6 servings (serving size: 1 filled crêpe).

CALORIES 272 (30% from fat); FAT 9.1g (sat 5g, mono 2.8g, poly 0.9g); PROTEIN 19.4g; CARB 27.5g; FIBER 0.8g; CHOL 66mg; IRON 2.1mg; SODIUM 643mg; CALC 66mg

Crêpes are paper-thin wrappers for sweet or savory fillings, and they are rolled up or folded over. Savory crêpes, such as these tasty rolls, are filled with meat, cheese, or vegetables and are often topped with a cream sauce. For convenience, buy prepackaged crêpes in the supermarket; look for them in refrigerated cases or in the produce department. Buy a prepackaged rotisserie chicken as well, and use the breast meat for this recipe. You'll have some leftover chicken you can use for another meal.

Hot Chicken and Chips Retro

To crush baked potato chips for the casserole topping, place the chips in a large zip-top plastic bag. With a meat mallet or rolling pin, crush the chips by lightly pounding or rolling until you achieve the desired size and texture. This method makes clean-up a breeze and keeps crumbs in the bag.

4 cups chopped roasted skinless, boneless chicken breast (about 4 breasts)
¼ cup chopped green onions
¼ cup chopped red bell pepper
2 tablespoons finely chopped fresh flat-leaf parsley
1 (8-ounce) can sliced water chestnuts, drained and chopped
½ cup low-fat mayonnaise
¼ cup reduced-fat sour cream
2 tablespoons fresh lemon juice
2 teaspoons Dijon mustard
½ teaspoon salt
½ teaspoon freshly ground black pepper
Cooking spray
¾ cup (3 ounces) shredded Swiss cheese
¾ cup crushed baked potato chips (about 2 ounces)

1. Preheat oven to 400°.
2. Combine chicken and next 4 ingredients in a large bowl; stir well. Combine low-fat mayonnaise and next 5 ingredients in a small bowl, stirring with a whisk. Add mayonnaise mixture to chicken mixture; stir well to combine. Spoon chicken mixture into an 11 x 7–inch baking dish coated with cooking spray; sprinkle with cheese. Top cheese evenly with chips. Bake at 400° for 13 minutes or until filling is bubbly and chips are golden. Yield: 6 servings.

CALORIES 321 (31% from fat); FAT 10.9g (sat 4.1g, mono 2.6g, poly 1g); PROTEIN 34.3g; CARB 20.4g; FIBER 2.6g; CHOL 96mg; IRON 11.4mg; SODIUM 606mg; CALC 175mg

This recipe has a nostalgic appeal that hearkens back to the 1950s and '60s. If you make it ahead, don't add the potato chips until it's time to bake the casserole, or they'll become soggy.

Caesar Chicken-Pasta Salad

3 cups (about 12 ounces)
shredded roasted skinless,
boneless chicken breast
(such as Tyson)

3 cups cooked penne (about
6 ounces uncooked
tube-shaped pasta)

2 cups thinly sliced romaine
lettuce

1½ cups halved grape or cherry
tomatoes

½ cup thinly sliced fresh basil

½ cup sliced green onions

⅓ cup fat-free Caesar dressing
(such as Cardini's)

¼ cup chopped fresh parsley

1 (4-ounce) package crumbled
feta cheese

1 garlic clove, minced

1. Combine all ingredients in a large bowl; toss well to coat. Yield: 4 servings (serving size: 2 cups).

Note: To lower the sodium in this dish, use plain cooked chicken in place of the commercial roasted variety, which is fairly high in sodium.

CALORIES 362 (22% from fat); FAT 8.8g (sat 5.2g, mono 1.4g, poly 0.6g); PROTEIN 19.4g; CARB 40.4g; FIBER 3.5g; CHOL 78mg; IRON 2.6mg; SODIUM 951mg; CALC 206mg

To shred roasted or cooked chicken, simply take two forks and pull the meat apart into bite-sized pieces. If not using the chicken immediately, store it, uncovered, in a shallow container in the refrigerator to help it cool quickly. Then cover the container when the chicken has cooled.

While this salad can be enjoyed the way it is, you can include or substitute different kinds of chicken, turkey, cheese, salad dressing, or herbs. It's the perfect mix-and-match meal.

Roasted-Chicken Noodle Soup

2 teaspoons olive oil
1 cup chopped onion
1 cup diced carrots
1 cup sliced celery
1 garlic clove, minced
¼ cup all-purpose flour
½ teaspoon dried oregano
¼ teaspoon dried thyme
¼ teaspoon poultry seasoning
6 cups fat-free, less-sodium chicken broth
4 cups diced peeled baking potato
1 teaspoon salt
2 cups shredded cooked chicken
1 cup evaporated fat-free milk
4 ounces (2 cups) uncooked wide egg noodles

1. Heat olive oil in a Dutch oven over medium heat. Add onion, carrots, celery, and garlic clove; sauté 5 minutes.
2. Lightly spoon flour into a dry measuring cup; level with a knife. Sprinkle flour, oregano, thyme, and poultry seasoning over vegetables, and cook 1 minute. Stir in broth, potato, and salt; bring to a boil. Reduce heat, and simmer, partially covered, 25 minutes or until potato is tender.
3. Add chicken, milk, and noodles, and cook 10 minutes or until noodles are tender. Yield: 8 servings (serving size: 1¼ cups).

CALORIES 247 (16% from fat); FAT 4.5g (sat 1.1g, mono 1.8g, poly 1g); PROTEIN 18g; CARB 32.8g; FIBER 2.9g; CHOL 46mg; IRON 2mg; SODIUM 701mg; CALC 71mg

Egg noodles differ from regular pasta in that they contain egg or egg yolks. They have a slightly higher fat content than other noodles. Egg noodles are usually short, flat noodles, but they may come in the form of fettuccine, tagliatelle, or other shapes. Because of their sturdy texture, they're often used in soups and casseroles, or they're paired with cream or meat sauces. Look for egg noodles in the pasta or bulk-food section of natural food or grocery stores. Store them, unopened, in a cool, dry cupboard for six to eight months. Two ounces (1 cup) uncooked wide egg noodles yields about 1 cup when cooked.

Classic chicken noodle soup consists of a clear broth, often cooked with small pieces of chicken, vegetables, noodles or dumplings, or grains such as rice and barley. We kicked the flavor and richness up a couple of notches by adding evaporated fat-free milk. Though we used a rotisserie chicken and canned broth to save time, this soup's health benefits remain intact.

dinner
tonight

Chicken Soft Tacos with Sautéed Onions and Apples

Granny Smith apples are our favorite apple for cooking, hands down. They remain tart, juicy, and crisp after baking. Try them in these flavorful chicken soft tacos. To achieve a tender texture, be sure to slice the apples so that they're very thin.

1 tablespoon olive oil
1 pound skinless, boneless chicken breast, cut into bite-sized pieces
½ teaspoon salt
½ teaspoon ground nutmeg
½ teaspoon freshly ground black pepper
1 tablespoon butter
2 cups thinly sliced onion
2 cups thinly sliced peeled Granny Smith apple (about 2 apples)
2 garlic cloves, minced
8 (6-inch) flour tortillas

1. Heat oil in a large nonstick skillet over medium-high heat. Sprinkle chicken evenly with salt, nutmeg, and pepper. Add chicken to pan; sauté 7 minutes or until golden. Remove chicken from pan; keep warm.

2. Melt butter in pan over medium heat. Add onion, and cook 4 minutes or until tender, stirring frequently. Add apple; cook 6 minutes or until golden, stirring frequently. Add garlic; sauté 30 seconds. Return chicken to pan; cook 2 minutes or until thoroughly heated, stirring frequently.

3. Heat tortillas according to package directions. Arrange ½ cup chicken mixture over each tortilla. Yield: 4 servings (serving size: 2 tacos).

CALORIES 454 (25% from fat); FAT 12.6g (sat 3.8g, mono 6.1g, poly 1.5g); PROTEIN 32.9g; CARB 51.5g; FIBER 4.8g; CHOL 73mg; IRON 3.3mg; SODIUM 705mg; CALC 116mg

And you thought that apples were only good in grandmother's apple pies! The unusual pairing of apples, chicken, onion, and nutmeg in this savory-sweet taco filling is divinely delicious.

Parmesan Chicken and Rice

Instant rice, also called pre-cooked rice, is rice that has been partially or completely cooked and dried; it takes only a few minutes to prepare. For instant rice, the ratio of rice to liquid is 1 to 1. One cup instant rice plus 1 cup liquid yields 2 cups cooked rice. For regular rice, 1 cup uncooked rice will yield about 3 cups cooked rice. As a general rule of thumb when cooking regular rice, use 2 cups of water per 1 cup of uncooked rice.

1 tablespoon olive oil
½ cup chopped onion
1 teaspoon bottled minced garlic
½ teaspoon dried thyme
1 (8-ounce) package presliced mushrooms
¾ pound skinless, boneless chicken breast, cut into bite-sized pieces
½ cup dry white wine
½ teaspoon salt
¼ teaspoon freshly ground black pepper
1 cup uncooked instant rice
1 cup fat-free, less-sodium chicken broth
½ cup (2 ounces) grated fresh Parmesan cheese
¼ cup chopped fresh parsley

1. Heat oil in a large nonstick skillet over medium-high heat. Add chopped onion, garlic, thyme, and mushrooms, and sauté 5 minutes or until onion is tender. Add chicken; sauté 4 minutes or until chicken is lightly browned. Add wine, salt, and pepper; cook 3 minutes or until liquid almost evaporates.
2. Stir in rice and broth. Bring to a boil; cover, reduce heat, and simmer 5 minutes or until liquid is absorbed. Stir in cheese and chopped parsley. Yield: 4 servings (serving size: about 1 cup).

CALORIES 395 (18% from fat); FAT 8g (sat 2.8g, mono 3.7g, poly 0.8g); PROTEIN 29.9g; CARB 44.4g; FIBER 2g; CHOL 57mg; IRON 4.1mg; SODIUM 656mg; CALC 171mg

Rice and broth are added to sautéed chicken, onion, garlic, and mushrooms for a simple entrée that requires only one pan.

Chicken with Rosemary Sauce

In Latin, rosemary means "dew of the sea," which is appropriate, since it is indigenous to the Mediterranean. Rosemary is one of the most aromatic and pungent of all herbs. Its needlelike leaves have a pronounced lemon-pine flavor that pairs well with olive oil and garlic. Rosemary is also a nice addition to focaccia, tomato sauce, pizza, chicken, lamb, and pork, but because its flavor is strong, use a light hand. Strip rosemary leaves from their tough, inedible stems by pulling in the opposite direction of the way the leaves grow.

8 ounces uncooked angel hair pasta
2 teaspoons olive oil
4 (6-ounce) skinless, boneless chicken breast halves
¼ teaspoon salt
⅛ teaspoon black pepper
½ cup chopped green onions
⅓ cup dry white wine
1 teaspoon minced fresh rosemary
½ cup fat-free, less-sodium chicken broth
⅓ cup whipping cream
2 tablespoons chopped green onions (optional)

1. Cook pasta according to package directions, omitting salt and fat.

2. While pasta cooks, heat oil in a large nonstick skillet over medium-high heat. Sprinkle chicken with salt and pepper. Add chicken to pan; cook 3 minutes on each side or until lightly browned. Add ½ cup onions, white wine, and rosemary; cook 30 seconds. Stir in broth; cook 2 minutes or until chicken is done. Add cream; cook 2 minutes. Garnish with 2 tablespoons green onions, if desired. Serve chicken and sauce over pasta. Yield: 4 servings (serving size: 1 chicken breast half, about 3 tablespoons sauce, and about 1 cup pasta).

CALORIES 480 (24% from fat); FAT 12.6g (sat 5.6g, mono 4.4g, poly 1.4g); PROTEIN 46.7g; CARB 41.3g; FIBER 2.9g; CHOL 126mg; IRON 3.3mg; SODIUM 328mg; CALC 44mg

Although quick and simple to prepare, the sauce made of wine, rosemary, and cream makes ordinary chicken breasts special. When served over pasta, you've got a complete meal.

Chicken with Provençal Sauce

4 (6-ounce) skinless, boneless chicken breast halves
¼ teaspoon salt
¼ teaspoon freshly ground black pepper
1½ tablespoons olive oil
1 garlic clove, minced
1 cup fat-free, less-sodium chicken broth
1½ teaspoons dried herbes de Provence
1 teaspoon fresh lemon juice
1 teaspoon butter
Thyme sprigs (optional)

1. Place each chicken breast half between 2 sheets of heavy-duty plastic wrap; pound to ½-inch thickness using a meat mallet or rolling pin. Sprinkle chicken evenly with salt and pepper.

2. Heat oil in a large nonstick skillet over medium heat. Add chicken; cook 6 minutes on each side or until done. Remove chicken from pan; keep warm.

3. Add garlic to pan; cook 1 minute, stirring constantly. Add broth and herbes de Provence; bring to a boil, scraping pan to loosen browned bits. Cook until broth mixture is reduced to ½ cup (about 3 minutes). Remove from heat; add lemon juice and butter, stirring until butter melts. Serve sauce over chicken. Garnish with thyme sprigs, if desired. Yield: 4 servings (serving size: 1 chicken breast half and about 2 tablespoons sauce).

CALORIES 248 (30% from fat); FAT 8.2g (sat 1.8g, mono 4.5g, poly 1g); PROTEIN 40.2g; CARB 1g; FIBER 0.3g; CHOL 101mg; IRON 1.5mg; SODIUM 376mg; CALC 32mg

Herbes de Provence is a mixture of dried herbs native to the Provence region of southern France. It traditionally contains rosemary, basil, bay leaves, and thyme. Other herbs, including savory, lavender, fennel seeds, and dried sage, are sometimes added. The proportion of the herbs in the mixture varies depending on the manufacturer. Herbes de Provence is used to flavor chicken, grilled meat, fish, and side dishes such as potatoes, rice, and pasta.

Capturing every morsel of chicken flavor is the secret to this quick-to-prepare dinner favorite. The tiny browned bits that remain in the skillet after the chicken is cooked are the key. Use the chicken broth to loosen these bits so that you don't leave any behind. Garlic, herbs, and fresh lemon juice are added for extra flavor. A final pat of butter marries these flavors into a slightly thickened sauce that is so intense that a couple of tablespoons is all that's needed to finish the dish.

Chicken with Pecan Cream and Mushrooms

¾ cup coarsely chopped
   pecans, toasted
1 cup water
1¼ teaspoons salt, divided
6 (6-ounce) skinless, boneless
   chicken breast halves
1 teaspoon freshly ground
   black pepper
Cooking spray
¼ cup finely chopped shallots
1 (8-ounce) package presliced
   mushrooms
4 cups cooked egg noodles
Chopped fresh parsley (optional)

1. Place pecans in a food processor; process until smooth (about 1 minute), scraping sides of bowl once. With processor on, add water and ¾ teaspoon salt; process until smooth, scraping sides of bowl once.

2. Sprinkle chicken with remaining ½ teaspoon salt and pepper.

3. Heat a large nonstick skillet over medium-high heat. Coat pan with cooking spray. Add chicken, and sauté 3 minutes on each side or until done. Remove chicken from pan, and keep warm.

4. Add shallots and mushrooms to pan; sauté 3 minutes or until mushrooms are tender. Stir in pecan cream; bring to a boil. Cook 1½ minutes. Place ⅔ cup noodles on each of 6 plates. Slice chicken; top each serving with 1 chicken breast half and ⅓ cup sauce. Garnish with parsley, if desired. Yield: 6 servings.

CALORIES 446 (29% from fat); FAT 14.5g (sat 1.8g, mono 7g, poly 4.2g); PROTEIN 47.1g; CARB 31.1g; FIBER 3.2g; CHOL 134mg; IRON 3.6mg; SODIUM 605mg; CALC 47mg

Nuts such as pecans, almonds, walnuts, and peanuts are a great way to add flavor to dishes without adding a lot of extra fat. The easiest way is to sprinkle a couple of tablespoons of chopped nuts over the dish just before serving. But if you want more intense nut flavor that permeates the whole dish, grind the nuts into a smooth butter or cream, and swirl into the sauce. We've found that a food processor works better than a blender for making nut butters. It takes about one minute to process ¾ cup of nuts to a smooth consistency.

A simple chicken sauté gets an elegant makeover. You can also serve it with rice or orzo to soak up the sauce. The sauce is also great made with almonds.

Chicken with Roasted Red Pepper Sauce

Bottled roasted red bell peppers can be packed in oil, but you'll find most are packed in water with a little vinegar. There may be a slight difference in flavor compared to fresh roasted red bell peppers, but the bottled variety is a convenient and tasty alternative.

2 bacon slices
4 (6-ounce) skinless, boneless chicken breast halves
¼ teaspoon salt
¼ teaspoon black pepper
½ cup chopped red onion
½ teaspoon ground coriander
3 garlic cloves, minced
1 drained canned chipotle chile in adobo sauce, diced
1 cup salsa
1 (7.5-ounce) bottle roasted red bell peppers, drained and sliced
Chopped fresh cilantro (optional)

1. Cook bacon in a large nonstick skillet over medium-high heat until crisp. Remove bacon from pan; crumble and set aside. Sprinkle chicken with salt and black pepper. Add chicken to bacon drippings in pan; sauté 2 minutes on each side. Remove chicken from pan. Add onion, coriander, garlic, and chile to pan; sauté 3 minutes. Stir in salsa and bell peppers. Return chicken to pan. Cover and cook over medium heat 12 minutes or until chicken is done. Sprinkle with crumbled bacon, and garnish with cilantro, if desired. Yield: 4 servings (serving size: 1 chicken breast half and ½ cup sauce).

CALORIES 259 (15% from fat); FAT 4.2g (sat 1g, mono 1.1g, poly 0.6g); PROTEIN 41.4g; CARB 10.8g; FIBER 0.8g; CHOL 102mg; IRON 1.7mg; SODIUM 982mg; CALC 49mg

You've heard the phrase "If you can't stand the heat, get out of the kitchen." Well, that best sums up this recipe. But if you love hot and spicy dishes, then this fiery recipe will heat things up. To curb some of the heat, you can always cut back on the chipotle chile or add some soothing sour cream. Try serving this dish with hearty chunks of bread or flour tortillas to soak up the sauce, if desired.

Lemon and Oregano–Rubbed Grilled Chicken

A Microplane® food grater is the ideal tool to use when a recipe calls for grated lemon rind or lemon zest. It's fast and efficient, and it removes only the intensely flavored yellow lemon rind without any of the white pith that is very bitter. But be careful—one slip can result in a scraped knuckle. You can also use a zester, handheld grater, or food processor. It's important not to use too much rind, which can add bitterness rather than tartness to a recipe. One medium lemon will yield about 1 teaspoon grated rind.

4 (6-ounce) skinless, boneless chicken breast halves
5 teaspoons grated lemon rind
1 tablespoon olive oil
1½ teaspoons dried oregano
¾ teaspoon kosher salt
½ teaspoon freshly ground black pepper
¼ teaspoon water
2 garlic cloves, minced
Cooking spray
4 lemon wedges
2 tablespoons chopped fresh parsley

1. Prepare grill.
2. Place each chicken breast half between 2 sheets of heavy-duty plastic wrap; pound to ¼-inch thickness using a meat mallet or rolling pin.
3. Combine lemon rind and next 6 ingredients, and rub evenly over both sides of chicken. Place chicken on a grill rack coated with cooking spray, and grill 3 minutes on each side or until done. Remove from heat. Squeeze 1 lemon wedge evenly over each chicken breast half. Sprinkle parsley evenly over chicken. Yield: 4 servings (serving size: 1 chicken breast half).

CALORIES 226 (22% from fat); FAT 5.6g (sat 1g, mono 3g, poly 0.8g); PROTEIN 39.6g; CARB 2.2g; FIBER 0.7g; CHOL 99mg; IRON 1.8mg; SODIUM 465mg; CALC 38mg

Pound the chicken breasts with a meat mallet or rolling pin until they're thin; the increased surface allows you to use even more of the flavorful rub. Using the pounding technique on the chicken not only tenderizes the meat but also shortens the cooking time and gives the appearance of a heartier portion.

Moroccan Chicken Thighs

Couscous, regarded by many as a grain, is actually pasta made from semolina (coarsely ground durum wheat). In some regions, however, couscous is made from coarsely ground barley or millet. Its earthy flavor is famously friendly to seasonings. And it's versatile, working well as a side dish, entrée, or salad.

  2 teaspoons olive oil
1½ pounds skinless, boneless chicken thighs, trimmed and cut into bite-sized pieces
  ½ cup chopped fresh cilantro
  ½ cup quartered dried Calimyrna figs (about 2 ounces)
  ¼ cup chopped green olives
  3 tablespoons sweet Marsala or Madeira
  2 tablespoons honey
  2 tablespoons balsamic vinegar
  1 tablespoon bottled minced garlic
  ½ teaspoon ground coriander
  ½ teaspoon ground cumin
  ¼ teaspoon ground cardamom
Cilantro sprigs (optional)
Couscous (optional)

1. Heat oil in a large nonstick skillet over medium-high heat. Add chicken; cook 5 minutes or until browned, stirring frequently. Stir in chopped cilantro and next 9 ingredients; reduce heat to medium, and cook 8 minutes or until chicken is done, stirring occasionally. Garnish with cilantro sprigs and serve with couscous, if desired. Yield: 4 servings (serving size: ¾ cup).

CALORIES 389 (39% from fat); FAT 16.7g (sat 4g, mono 7.2g, poly 3.3g); PROTEIN 31.6g; CARB 27.6g; FIBER 3g; CHOL 112mg; IRON 2.7mg; SODIUM 183mg; CALC 72mg

This Moroccan-inspired chicken dish is best served over a bed of fluffy, yellow couscous. Couscous, which is central to Moroccan cuisine, is often cooked with spices, vegetables, nuts, and raisins and topped with rich stews and roasted meats. Morocco, the culinary star of North Africa, is the doorway between Europe and Africa. Unlike the herb-based cooking to the north, Moroccan cooking features rich spices, including cumin, coriander, saffron, chiles, dried ginger, cinnamon, and paprika.

Chicken with Green Olives

Adding olives to your meals not only enhances the flavor but also helps your heart. Between 75 and 85 percent of the caloric content of olives is monounsaturated fat, which, when replacing saturated fat in the diet, can help lower your cholesterol levels. The monounsaturated fat in olives helps lower LDL (the "bad" cholesterol) levels and also prevents the buildup of plaque along artery walls. However, if you are on a low-sodium diet, you should be mindful that some olives may be high in sodium.

1 tablespoon olive oil
8 bone-in chicken thighs (about 2¼ pounds), skinned
¾ teaspoon black pepper, divided
¼ teaspoon salt
2 cups chopped onion
1 tablespoon minced fresh garlic
2 teaspoons minced peeled fresh ginger
1 teaspoon ground cumin
1 teaspoon paprika
½ teaspoon ground turmeric
Dash of ground red pepper
1 (3-inch) cinnamon stick
1 bay leaf
2 cups fat-free, less-sodium chicken broth
⅔ cup pitted green olives
2 tablespoons fresh lemon juice
¼ cup chopped fresh cilantro
3 cups hot cooked couscous

1. Heat olive oil in a large nonstick skillet over medium-high heat. Sprinkle chicken with ¼ teaspoon black pepper and ¼ teaspoon salt. Add chicken to pan; cook 10 minutes, browning on all sides. Remove chicken from pan; reduce heat to medium.
2. Add remaining ½ teaspoon black pepper, onion, and next 8 ingredients; cook 5 minutes, stirring occasionally. Add broth; bring to a boil. Return chicken to pan, and reduce heat. Simmer, uncovered, 15 minutes or until chicken is done. Discard cinnamon stick and bay leaf.
3. While chicken cooks, place olives in a small saucepan, and cover with water. Bring to a boil, and drain. Repeat procedure. Add olives and lemon juice to chicken mixture, and sprinkle with cilantro. Serve over couscous. Yield: 4 servings (serving size: 2 chicken thighs, ½ cup sauce, and ¾ cup couscous).

CALORIES 486 (37% from fat); FAT 19.8g (sat 4.5g, mono 9.8g, poly 3.6g); PROTEIN 37.1g; CARB 39.3g; FIBER 4g; CHOL 109mg; IRON 2.8mg; SODIUM 890mg; CALC 65mg

This North African dish is also served in southern Spain and Italy. Traditionally, it's made as a stew because the region's farm-raised chickens require long cooking for tenderness. This version calls for flavorful chicken thighs that cook quickly. Lightly blanching the olives brings out the true flavor by removing the briny overtones. This dish becomes even more flavorful with time, so don't hesitate to make it early in the day or the night before and reheat just before serving.

(pictured on cover)

Chicken with Prosciutto and Tomatoes over Polenta

Native to the northern Mediterranean coast, sage is used often in the region's cuisine. Sage's long, narrow leaves have a distinctively fuzzy texture and a musty flavor. Sage is available either fresh or in three dried forms: ground, coarsely crumbled, or rubbed (finely chopped). While the flavor of fresh herbs is generally much better than that of dried, sometimes fresh is not available, so quality dried herbs are an important part of a basic pantry.

4 bone-in chicken thighs (about 1⅛ pounds), skinned
1 tablespoon chopped fresh or 1 teaspoon dried rubbed sage
¼ teaspoon salt, divided
¼ teaspoon freshly ground black pepper
½ cup all-purpose flour
2 teaspoons olive oil
½ cup dry white wine
⅔ cup yellow cornmeal
2 cups water
1 cup chopped seeded peeled tomato
1 teaspoon fresh lemon juice
2 very thin slices prosciutto or ham, cut into thin strips (about ¼ cup)
Sage sprigs (optional)

1. Sprinkle chicken with chopped sage, ⅛ teaspoon salt, and pepper. Place flour in a shallow dish. Dredge chicken in flour. Heat oil in a nonstick skillet over medium-high heat. Add chicken; cook 4 minutes on each side. Add wine; cover, reduce heat, and simmer 20 minutes or until a meat thermometer registers 180°.

2. Place cornmeal and remaining ⅛ teaspoon salt in a 1-quart casserole. Gradually add water, stirring until blended. Cover. Microwave at HIGH 12 minutes, stirring every 3 minutes. Let stand, covered, 5 minutes.

3. Remove chicken from pan. Add tomato to pan; cook 1 minute. Stir in lemon juice and prosciutto. Spoon polenta onto plates; top with chicken. Serve with tomato sauce. Garnish with sage sprigs, if desired. Yield: 2 servings (serving size: 2 thighs, ½ cup polenta, and ½ cup sauce).

CALORIES 594 (30% from fat); FAT 20g (sat 4.9g, mono 8.4g, poly 3.8g); PROTEIN 41.2g; CARB 64.2g; FIBER 4.6g; CHOL 116mg; IRON 5.2mg; SODIUM 656mg; CALC 41mg

When it comes to great chicken flavor, thighs rule. Cheap and tasty, chicken thighs can go fancy or simple. And they can be quick and easy, too. Just prepare the polenta while the chicken cooks, and you've got dinner tonight in no time.

one-dish meals

Chicken Tetrazzini

Parmesan is full of flavor, so a little is sure to go a long way. For the best flavor, buy the real thing, which has Parmigiano-Reggiano printed on the rind. It has a sharper flavor and a texture that is more easily crumbled than that of domestic Parmesan. But the distinctive flavor and texture of Parmigiano-Reggiano is pricey. The domestic versions can work just as well in recipes, but the cheese flavor will not be as sharp.

1 tablespoon butter
Cooking spray
1 cup finely chopped onion
⅔ cup finely chopped celery
1 teaspoon freshly ground black pepper
¾ teaspoon salt
3 (8-ounce) packages presliced mushrooms
½ cup dry sherry
⅔ cup all-purpose flour
3 (14-ounce) cans fat-free, less-sodium chicken broth
2¼ cups (9 ounces) shredded fresh Parmesan cheese, divided
½ cup (4 ounces) block-style ⅓-less-fat cream cheese
7 cups hot cooked vermicelli (about 1 pound uncooked pasta)
4 cups chopped cooked chicken breast (about 1½ pounds)
1 (1-ounce) slice white bread

1. Preheat oven to 350°.
2. Melt butter in a large stockpot coated with cooking spray over medium-high heat. Add onion, celery, pepper, salt, and mushrooms, and sauté 4 minutes or until mushrooms are tender. Add sherry; cook 1 minute.
3. Lightly spoon flour into dry measuring cups; level with a knife. Gradually add flour to pan; cook 3 minutes, stirring constantly with a whisk (mixture will be thick). Gradually add broth, stirring constantly. Bring to a boil. Reduce heat; simmer 5 minutes, stirring frequently. Remove from heat.
4. Add 1¾ cups Parmesan cheese and cream cheese, stirring with a whisk until cream cheese melts. Add pasta and chicken, and stir until blended. Divide pasta mixture between 2 (8-inch square) baking dishes coated with cooking spray.
5. Place bread in a food processor, and pulse 10 times or until coarse crumbs form. Combine breadcrumbs and remaining ½ cup Parmesan cheese, and sprinkle evenly over pasta mixture.
6. Bake at 350° for 30 minutes or until lightly browned. Remove from oven; let stand 15 minutes. Yield: 2 casseroles, 6 servings each (serving size: about 1⅓ cups).

CALORIES 380 (29% from fat); FAT 12.2g (sat 6.6g, mono 3.4g, poly 0.7g); PROTEIN 33g; CARB 32.7g; FIBER 2g; CHOL 66mg; IRON 2.8mg; SODIUM 964mg; CALC 319mg

Named after opera singer Luisa Tetrazzini, Chicken Tetrazzini combines cooked vermicelli, chicken, and mushrooms with a rich sherry–Parmesan cheese sauce. The mixture is sprinkled with breadcrumbs and Parmesan cheese and baked until bubbly and golden. This is a great way to use leftover cooked chicken or turkey.

Mediterranean Chicken with Potatoes

Sometimes called new potatoes, small, young red potatoes haven't had time to become starchy. Because of this, they have a waxy texture that makes them good for boiling and making potato salad, or for pan-roasting. They are usually available from spring to early summer and should be used within two or three days after you purchase them.

4 teaspoons minced garlic, divided
1 tablespoon olive oil
1 teaspoon salt, divided
¼ teaspoon dried thyme
½ teaspoon black pepper, divided
12 small red potatoes, halved (about 1½ pounds)
Cooking spray
2 pounds skinless, boneless chicken breast, cut into bite-sized pieces
1 cup vertically sliced red onion
¾ cup dry white wine
¾ cup fat-free, less-sodium chicken broth
½ cup chopped pepperoncini peppers
¼ cup pitted kalamata olives, halved
2 cups chopped plum tomato
2 tablespoons chopped fresh basil
1 (14-ounce) can artichoke hearts, drained and quartered
½ cup (2 ounces) grated fresh Parmesan cheese
Thyme sprigs (optional)

1. Preheat oven to 400°.
2. Combine 2 teaspoons garlic, oil, ¼ teaspoon salt, thyme, ¼ teaspoon black pepper, and potatoes on a jelly-roll pan coated with cooking spray. Bake at 400° for 30 minutes or until tender.
3. Heat a large Dutch oven over medium-high heat. Coat pan with cooking spray. Sprinkle chicken with ½ teaspoon salt and remaining ¼ teaspoon black pepper. Add half of chicken to pan; sauté 5 minutes or until browned. Remove chicken from pan. Repeat procedure with remaining chicken; remove from pan.
4. Add onion to pan; sauté 5 minutes. Stir in wine, scraping pan to loosen browned bits. Bring wine to a boil; cook until reduced to ⅓ cup (about 2 minutes). Add potatoes, chicken, broth, pepperoncini peppers, and olives; cook 3 minutes, stirring occasionally. Stir in remaining 2 teaspoons garlic, remaining ¼ teaspoon salt, tomato, basil, and artichokes, and cook 3 minutes or until thoroughly heated. Sprinkle with cheese. Garnish with thyme sprigs, if desired. Yield: 8 servings (serving size: 1¼ cups).

CALORIES 331 (20% from fat); FAT 7.3g (sat 2.1g, mono 3.7g, poly 0.9g); PROTEIN 33.5g; CARB 32.5g; FIBER 3.6g; CHOL 71mg; IRON 2.9mg; SODIUM 897mg; CALC 124mg

The small red potatoes in this dish are roasted in the oven to give them a deep caramelized flavor before they're tossed with the other ingredients. A Greek salad makes a great accompaniment to this wonderful blend of flavors and textures. A crusty bread loaf and a good bottle of wine are all you need to round out the meal.

Fragrant Chicken in Creamy Almond Sauce

Unlike ground spices and herbs, which are usually added to a recipe close to the end of the cooking time, whole spices and herbs such as cinnamon sticks and bay leaves are added at the beginning of the recipe. The long cook time gives oils in the cinnamon and bay leaves time to escape into the liquid. By the time the dish is finished, all the flavor has been extracted, and it's time to discard the spices and herbs before serving. Occasionally, recipes tell you to heat or toast whole spices and herbs in a hot skillet before adding them to the recipe. This method releases their flavors as soon as they're added to the pot.

1 tablespoon olive oil
6 (3-inch) cinnamon sticks
5 bay leaves
1½ cups finely chopped onion
6 garlic cloves, minced
2 teaspoons curry powder
½ teaspoon ground turmeric
½ teaspoon salt
¼ teaspoon ground cardamom
2½ pounds skinless, boneless chicken breast, cut into 1-inch pieces
1 cup fat-free, less-sodium chicken broth
¼ cup fat-free sour cream
1 teaspoon all-purpose flour
½ teaspoon sugar
¼ cup slivered almonds, toasted and ground
⅓ cup chopped red bell pepper
2 tablespoons slivered almonds, toasted
Cinnamon sticks (optional)
Hot cooked basmati rice (optional)

1. Heat oil in a large nonstick skillet over medium heat. Add 6 cinnamon sticks and bay leaves. Cook 2 minutes or until fragrant. Add chopped onion and garlic, and sauté 5 minutes or until tender. Add curry powder, turmeric, salt, and cardamom. Add chicken and broth, and bring to a boil. Cover, reduce heat, and simmer 35 minutes or until chicken is tender.

2. Remove chicken from pan with a slotted spoon. Cook liquid remaining in pan over low heat 5 minutes. Combine sour cream, flour, and sugar in a small bowl; stir in ½ cup hot liquid. Add sour cream mixture to pan, stirring until smooth. Return chicken to pan; stir in ground almonds. Cook 5 minutes or until thick, stirring frequently. Sprinkle with bell pepper. Remove and discard cinnamon sticks and bay leaves. Sprinkle with slivered almonds; garnish with cinnamon sticks and serve with rice, if desired. Yield: 6 servings (serving size: about 1 cup chicken mixture and 1 teaspoon almonds).

CALORIES 304 (23% from fat); FAT 7.9g (sat 1.3g, mono 4.2g, poly 1.3g); PROTEIN 46.9g; CARB 8.7g; FIBER 2.1g; CHOL 110mg; IRON 2.4mg; SODIUM 410mg; CALC 60mg

Indulge your sense of smell with this delicious, beautiful, and fantastically fragrant dish. While very creamy and decadent, it's not too rich or heavy. If you are accustomed to heavily seasoned Indian-style dishes, you may want to increase the amount of curry powder to give it a little extra kick.

Chicken Fricassee

3 tablespoons all-purpose flour
1 teaspoon paprika
1 teaspoon poultry seasoning
½ teaspoon salt
½ teaspoon black pepper
4 (8-ounce) bone-in chicken breast halves, skinned
2 teaspoons butter
1½ cups chopped onion
½ cup chopped celery
3 garlic cloves, minced
1 cup fat-free, less-sodium chicken broth
⅓ cup dry white wine
2 cups (3-inch) julienne-cut carrot
¼ cup chopped fresh parsley
Hot cooked long-grain rice (optional)

1. Combine first 5 ingredients in a large zip-top plastic bag. Add chicken; toss well to coat. Remove chicken from bag; reserve flour mixture. Melt butter in a large nonstick skillet over medium heat. Add chicken, breast sides down; sauté 5 minutes or until chicken is browned. Remove chicken from pan; keep warm.
2. Add onion, celery, and garlic to pan; sauté 5 to 7 minutes, stirring occasionally. Stir in reserved flour mixture, and cook 1 minute. Add broth and wine; bring to a boil. Add carrot. Return chicken to pan, breast sides up. Cover, reduce heat, and simmer 25 minutes or until chicken is done. Sprinkle with chopped parsley. Serve over rice, if desired. Yield: 4 servings (serving size: 1 chicken breast half and ¾ cup sauce).

CALORIES 265 (14% from fat); FAT 4.1g (sat 1.9g, mono 0.5g, poly 0.6g); PROTEIN 37g; CARB 19g; FIBER 3.4g; CHOL 91mg; IRON 2.4mg; SODIUM 600mg; CALC 71mg

A julienne cut (also called a "matchstick") is a type of cut that makes a long, thin strip. It's a good technique to use for vegetables when you want to heighten their presentation. Julienned vegetables can also be used as a garnish. A sharp, nonserrated kitchen knife, such as a chef's knife, makes the best cuts. Avoid serrated knives, which saw through food. The ideal julienne cut is about 2 inches long—any longer and it's hard to get the vegetable into your mouth. If the vegetable is round like a carrot or potato, cut it in half and lay it on the cutting board cut side down. This will keep it from rolling so that you can make even slices.

Chicken Fricassee sounds upscale. In reality, it's the ultimate comfort food—a creamy dish of succulent chicken and tender vegetables smothered in a rich brown gravy that's best when spooned over mashed potatoes, rice, or even grits. Bone-in chicken pieces are essential, as the bones contribute depth of flavor to the overall dish. Braising—slow simmering in moist heat in a covered skillet—is the key to a good fricassee with tender chicken and thickened juices. First, the chicken is panfried in a little butter until brown and crisp. After the vegetables have cooked a bit, the chicken is added back to the pan with broth, wine, or a combination of the two. The pan is covered, and the chicken simmers in moist heat until it becomes tender and the juices thicken.

Chicken and Rosemary Dumplings

Americans are both passionate and opinionated about chicken and dumplings. The dumplings *must* be rolled, or they *must* be dropped. In this recipe, the dumplings are dropped. Using two spoons, drop the sticky dumpling dough, 1 tablespoon per dumpling, into the chicken mixture to form 12 dumplings.

Soup:
4 cups fat-free, less-sodium chicken broth
3 cups water
1 pound chicken drumsticks, skinned
1 pound skinless, boneless chicken breast halves
2 thyme sprigs
2 teaspoons olive oil
1½ cups diced carrot
1½ cups chopped celery
1 cup diced onion
2 garlic cloves, minced
½ teaspoon salt

Dumplings:
1¼ cups all-purpose flour
1 tablespoon chopped fresh or ½ teaspoon dried rosemary
2 teaspoons baking powder
¼ teaspoon salt
2 tablespoons butter, softened
½ cup low-fat buttermilk
1 large egg, lightly beaten

Remaining Ingredients:
¼ cup all-purpose flour
¼ cup water
Freshly ground black pepper

1. To prepare soup, combine first 5 ingredients in a large Dutch oven over medium-high heat; bring to a boil. Reduce heat, and simmer, uncovered, 15 minutes or until chicken is done. Remove pan from heat. Remove chicken pieces from broth; cool slightly. Strain broth through a sieve into a large bowl; discard solids. Remove chicken from bones. Discard bones; chop chicken into bite-sized pieces. Set chicken aside.

2. Heat oil in pan over medium-high heat. Add carrot, celery, onion, and garlic; sauté 6 minutes or until onion is tender. Add reserved broth mixture and ½ teaspoon salt; simmer 10 minutes. Keep warm.

3. To prepare dumplings, lightly spoon 1¼ cups flour into dry measuring cups; level with a knife. Combine 1¼ cups flour, rosemary, baking powder, and ¼ teaspoon salt in a large bowl. Cut in butter with a pastry blender or 2 knives until mixture resembles coarse meal. Combine buttermilk and egg, stirring with a whisk. Add buttermilk mixture to flour mixture, stirring just until combined.

4. Add chicken to broth mixture; bring to a simmer over medium-high heat. Lightly spoon ¼ cup flour into a dry measuring cup; level with a knife. Combine flour and ¼ cup water, stirring with a whisk until well blended to form a slurry. Add slurry to pan; simmer 3 minutes. Drop dumpling dough, 1 tablespoon per dumpling, into chicken mixture to form 12 dumplings. Cover and cook 7 minutes (do not let broth boil). Sprinkle with pepper. Yield: 6 servings (serving size: 2 dumplings and 1⅓ cups soup).

CALORIES 366 (24% from fat); FAT 9.7g (sat 3.8g, mono 3.5g, poly 1.3g); PROTEIN 32.5g; CARB 35.1g; FIBER 2.9g; CHOL 115mg; IRON 3.3mg; SODIUM 936mg; CALC 169mg

Spoonfuls of seasoned buttermilk biscuit dough form light, fluffy dumplings in this classic American dish.

Arroz con Pollo

Arroz con pollo comes in many variations; however, it always starts with *sofrito*—a sautéed mixture of onion, bell pepper, and garlic. Sofrito is often the first aroma you smell when you enter a Spanish, Mexican, or South American home. To make sofrito, add onion, bell pepper, and garlic to a pan. Cover and cook 10 minutes or until tender. When complete, you've got a good base for your chicken-and-rice recipe.

6 chicken drumsticks (about 1½ pounds), skinned
6 bone-in chicken thighs (about 2 pounds), skinned
1½ teaspoons dried oregano, divided
½ teaspoon salt
¼ teaspoon freshly ground black pepper
1 tablespoon vegetable oil
2 tablespoons fresh lime juice
1 cup chopped onion
½ cup chopped green bell pepper
2 garlic cloves, minced
1 teaspoon ground turmeric
¾ teaspoon ground cumin
1½ cups uncooked Arborio rice
½ cup diced ham
2¼ cups fat-free, less-sodium chicken broth
1 (14.5-ounce) can diced tomatoes, undrained
½ cup frozen petite green peas, thawed
½ cup chopped pimiento-stuffed green olives

1. Sprinkle chicken with 1 teaspoon oregano, salt, and black pepper. Heat oil in a Dutch oven over medium-high heat. Add chicken; cook 8 minutes, browning on all sides. Remove chicken from pan; drizzle with lime juice. Cover; keep warm.

2. Add onion, bell pepper, and garlic to pan. Cover, reduce heat to low, and cook 10 minutes or until tender. Stir in remaining ½ teaspoon oregano, turmeric, and cumin, and sauté 1 minute. Stir in rice and ham; cook 1 minute. Increase heat to medium. Add broth and tomatoes; bring to a boil. Add chicken, nestling into rice mixture. Cover, reduce heat, and simmer 18 minutes or until liquid is almost absorbed and chicken is done. Stir in peas; cover and cook 3 minutes. Remove from heat, and let stand, uncovered, 5 minutes. Sprinkle with olives. Yield: 6 servings (serving size: 1 drumstick, 1 thigh, and 1 cup rice mixture).

CALORIES 405 (33% from fat); FAT 14.7g (sat 3.5g, mono 6g, poly 3.6g); PROTEIN 38.8g; CARB 28.2g; FIBER 2.9g; CHOL 119mg; IRON 2.9mg; SODIUM 853mg; CALC 53mg

Literally translated as "rice and chicken," Arroz con Pollo is a Spanish and Mexican dish that usually includes chicken, rice, tomatoes, green bell peppers, and seasonings. Sometimes saffron is also added. We use turmeric to color the rice yellow; other versions use annatto seeds or saffron.

Braised Root Vegetables and Chicken Thighs

Parsnips are similar in shape to carrots, but they taper more and are creamy white rather than orange in color. Parsnips have a flavor that's described as nutty, spicy, or peppery. They are suited to prolonged cooking, so they're great for casseroles and stews. Select firm, unshriveled parsnips of moderate size (large ones can be woody). The outside should be relatively clean and free of surface blemishes. Parsnips will store well for several weeks in plastic packaging in your refrigerator's vegetable crisper. Before using parsnips, rinse well, trim the crown, and peel the outer skin.

¼ cup all-purpose flour
8 bone-in chicken thighs (about 2¼ pounds), skinned
5 teaspoons olive oil, divided
2 cups chopped onion
2 cups (¾-inch) cubed peeled rutabaga
2 cups (¾-inch) cubed peeled turnip (about 1 pound)
2 cups (¾-inch) cubed peeled butternut squash
1 cup (¼-inch-thick) slices parsnip
1 garlic clove, minced
½ cup fat-free, less-sodium chicken broth
1 teaspoon chopped fresh or ¼ teaspoon dried thyme
1 teaspoon chopped fresh or ¼ teaspoon dried rubbed sage
½ teaspoon salt
¼ teaspoon black pepper
1 bay leaf

1. Place flour in a shallow dish; dredge chicken in flour.
2. Heat 1 tablespoon oil in a large nonstick skillet over medium-high heat. Add chicken; sauté 5 minutes, turning once. Remove chicken from pan, and keep warm.
3. Heat remaining 2 teaspoons oil in pan. Add onion; sauté 3 minutes. Add rutabaga, turnip, squash, parsnip, and garlic; sauté 3 minutes. Stir in broth and next 5 ingredients, and nestle chicken into vegetable mixture. Bring to a boil; cover, reduce heat, and simmer 20 minutes or until chicken is done. Uncover and simmer 3 minutes or until thick. Remove bay leaf. Yield: 4 servings (serving size: 2 thighs and 1¼ cups vegetable mixture).

CALORIES 477 (35% from fat); FAT 18.6g (sat 4.3g, mono 8.9g, poly 3.6g); PROTEIN 34.7g; CARB 44g; FIBER 5.2g; CHOL 109mg; IRON 3.7mg; SODIUM 531mg; CALC 158mg

Winter is the peak season for parsnips, rutabagas, and turnips. Their strong flavors, along with that of the chicken thighs, mellow while cooking and make this a quintessential hearty cold-weather meal. Garnish with a fresh bay leaf for a simple, elegant presentation.

Colonel Benjamin's Curry Chicken

A Dutch oven is neither Dutch nor an oven; rather, it's a deep pot with a tight-fitting lid that can go from cooktop to oven. It usually holds 3 to 6 quarts. Some versions come with a long handle, like a skillet. Dutch ovens are frequently used for braising and for making soups, stews, chilis, pot roasts, and pasta.

1 teaspoon salt
1 teaspoon ground coriander
1 teaspoon ground cumin
1 teaspoon chili powder
1 teaspoon grated peeled fresh ginger
¼ teaspoon ground turmeric
1 teaspoon canola oil
4 cups finely chopped onion
2 garlic cloves, minced
3½ cups coarsely chopped peeled tomato (about 1½ pounds)
2 tablespoons fresh lemon juice
12 bone-in chicken thighs (about 3 pounds), skinned
½ teaspoon salt
1½ pounds peeled baking potato, cut into 1-inch pieces
2 tablespoons chopped fresh cilantro
3 cups hot cooked rice
Cilantro sprigs

1. Combine first 6 ingredients.
2. Heat oil in a Dutch oven over medium-high heat. Add onion and garlic, and cook 15 minutes, stirring frequently. Add cumin mixture, tomato, and lemon juice. Reduce heat to medium, and cook 10 minutes, stirring occasionally.
3. Sprinkle chicken with ½ teaspoon salt. Add chicken and potato to pan; stir in chopped cilantro. Bring to a boil; cover, reduce heat, and simmer 50 minutes or until chicken is done. Serve over rice, and garnish with cilantro sprigs. Yield: 6 servings (serving size: 2 thighs, 1 cup potato curry, and ½ cup rice).

CALORIES 479 (24% from fat); FAT 12.6g (sat 3.3g, mono 4.8g, poly 3g); PROTEIN 32.7g; CARB 58.5g; FIBER 4.5g; CHOL 97mg; IRON 3.6mg; SODIUM 704mg; CALC 69mg

Enjoy the intoxicating aromas of Indian cuisine with this century-old recipe. The spices meld well with the flavor from the chicken thighs in this traditional Indian chicken dish from the kitchen of Colonel Benjamin, a retiree from the Indian Army. This dish is a must for curry-lovers.

Easy Bistro Chicken

Keep kitchen shears handy to chop the Italian-style tomatoes. This method saves time and is far less messy than chopping them on a cutting board. No kitchen or cook should be without this handy tool.

2 tablespoons olive oil, divided
4 (8-ounce) bone-in chicken breast halves, skinned
4 bone-in chicken thighs (about 1½ pounds), skinned
4 chicken drumsticks (about 1 pound), skinned
2 cups chopped onion
4 garlic cloves, minced
1 cup chopped celery
½ cup chopped fresh basil
½ cup chopped fresh flat-leaf parsley
½ cup red wine vinegar
¼ cup sliced green olives
¼ cup capers
1 tablespoon sugar
Dash of ground red pepper
2 bay leaves
1 (28-ounce) can Italian-style tomatoes, undrained and chopped
8 cups hot cooked macaroni or cavatappi
Flat-leaf parsley sprigs (optional)

1. Heat 1½ teaspoons oil in a large nonstick skillet over medium-high heat. Add chicken breast halves to pan; sauté 2 minutes on each side or until lightly browned. Remove from pan. Add 1½ teaspoons oil and remaining chicken pieces; sauté 2 minutes on each side or until lightly browned. Remove chicken from pan.
2. Heat remaining 1 tablespoon oil in pan. Add onion and garlic; sauté 5 minutes. Add celery; sauté 5 minutes. Add basil and next 8 ingredients. Return chicken to pan; bring to a boil. Cover, reduce heat, and simmer 20 minutes.
3. Uncover and simmer 25 minutes or until chicken is tender. Discard bay leaves. Serve with pasta. Garnish with parsley sprigs, if desired. Yield: 8 servings (serving size: 1 chicken breast half or 1 thigh and 1 drumstick, ½ cup sauce, and 1 cup pasta).

CALORIES 485 (21% from fat); FAT 11.5g (sat 2.5g, mono 5.4g, poly 2.3g); PROTEIN 41.9g; CARB 50.3g; FIBER 4g; CHOL 101mg; IRON 6.2mg; SODIUM 471mg; CALC 90mg

Cozy up to a blazing fire on a cold winter's night with Easy Bistro Chicken. You'll find it's reminiscent of a cacciatore. Italian for "hunter," cacciatore is a stewlike dish flavored with onions, herbs, mushrooms, tomatoes, and sometimes wine.

Chicken, Date, and Apricot Tagine

A good set of kitchen knives is a must-have for any cook's kitchen. For this particular recipe, both a chef's knife and a paring knife come in handy. Use a chef's knife to cut up the chicken, onion, fruit, and herbs, and use a small paring knife to section the lemon and remove the strips of rind. If using the same knife to cut both the chicken and other ingredients, be sure to wash it in hot soapy water after cutting the chicken to prevent foodborne illness.

1 (3-pound) broiler-fryer
   chicken
1 tablespoon olive oil
1 cup chopped onion
1 teaspoon ground turmeric
1 teaspoon ground cumin
½ teaspoon ground ginger
½ teaspoon ground cinnamon
⅛ teaspoon ground red
   pepper
5 garlic cloves, minced
1½ cups fat-free, less-sodium
   chicken broth
⅓ cup sliced whole pitted
   dates
⅓ cup sliced dried apricots
2 teaspoons (1-inch) julienne-
   cut lemon rind
½ teaspoon salt
⅓ cup chopped fresh parsley
⅓ cup lemon sections, peeled
   and chopped
2 tablespoons chopped fresh
   cilantro
3 cups hot cooked couscous

1. Skin and cut chicken into 2 drumsticks, 2 thighs, 2 breast halves, and 2 wings. Reserve chicken wings for another use. Discard back and giblets.
2. Heat oil in a Dutch oven over medium-high heat. Add chicken; cook 5 minutes on each side or until browned. Add onion and next 6 ingredients; cook 4 minutes, stirring occasionally. Add broth, dates, apricots, rind, and salt. Bring to a boil; cover, reduce heat, and simmer 30 minutes or until chicken is tender. Remove from heat; stir in parsley, lemon sections, and cilantro. Serve over couscous. Yield: 4 servings (serving size: 1 breast half or 1 thigh and 1 drumstick, ¾ cup fruit mixture, and ¾ cup couscous).

CALORIES 473 (17% from fat); FAT 8.7g (sat 1.7g, mono 4g, poly 1.7g); PROTEIN 42.9g; CARB 55.6g; FIBER 5.4g; CHOL 113mg; IRON 4mg; SODIUM 648mg; CALC 77mg

For centuries, nomads in Morocco and North Africa have used portable cone-topped clay cookers called tagines to make their traditional stews. Updated versions of these classic stews are made in Dutch ovens. The recipes, which are basically slow-cooked meats with fruit and vegetables, are actually called tagines as well. Serve over hot cooked couscous for the ultimate one-dish meal.

on the grill

Chicken Saté with Peanut Sauce

Bamboo skewers, an alternative to metal skewers, get hot quickly and can burn. To help prevent this, count out the number of skewers needed for the recipe. Place the skewers in a baking dish or pan, and cover with warm water. Soak the skewers for 30 minutes prior to use.

Saté:
1½ pounds skinless, boneless chicken breast, cut into 8 strips
1 tablespoon light brown sugar
2½ tablespoons low-sodium soy sauce
2 teaspoons bottled ground fresh ginger (such as Spice World)
1 teaspoon grated lime rind
¼ teaspoon crushed red pepper
2 garlic cloves, minced

Sauce:
1 tablespoon light brown sugar
1½ tablespoons low-sodium soy sauce
2 tablespoons natural-style, reduced-fat creamy peanut butter (such as Smucker's)
1 tablespoon fresh lime juice
¼ teaspoon crushed red pepper
1 garlic clove, minced

Remaining Ingredients:
Cooking spray
Wide rice noodles (optional)

1. Prepare grill.

2. To prepare saté, combine chicken and next 6 ingredients in a medium bowl. Let stand 10 minutes.

3. To prepare sauce, combine 1 tablespoon brown sugar and next 5 ingredients in a medium bowl, stirring until sugar dissolves.

4. Thread chicken strips onto each of 8 (8-inch) skewers. Place chicken on grill rack coated with cooking spray; grill 5 minutes on each side or until done. Serve chicken with sauce. Serve with wide rice noodles, if desired. Yield: 4 servings (serving size: 2 skewers and 1 tablespoon sauce).
Note: If using wooden skewers, soak them in water 30 minutes before grilling.

CALORIES 269 (17% from fat); FAT 5.2g (sat 1.2g, mono 0.5g, poly 0.5g); PROTEIN 42.4g; CARB 11.4g; FIBER 0.9g; CHOL 99mg; IRON 2mg; SODIUM 709mg; CALC 32mg

You can broil these chicken skewers instead of grilling them. In fact, traditional Indonesian saté skewers are often broiled. Place on a broiler pan coated with cooking spray; broil 8 to 10 minutes, turning once. Serve the zesty peanut sauce in condiment bowls on individual serving plates.

Mediterranean Chicken and Vegetable Kebabs

With its rounded pale green bulb, short stems, and feathery green leaves, fennel is easily mistaken for a bunch of plump celery. But its mild, sweet flavor, which is akin to licorice or anise, sets it apart. Look for small, heavy white fennel bulbs that are firm and free of cracks, browning, or moist areas. The stalks should be crisp, with feathery bright green fronds. Trim the stalks about an inch above the bulb. Keep the root end intact so the wedges will hold together as they're threaded on the skewer.

½ cup fresh lemon juice
3 tablespoons fresh chopped or 1 tablespoon dried oregano
3 tablespoons olive oil
2 garlic cloves, minced
1½ pounds skinless, boneless chicken breast, cut into 32 (1½-inch) cubes
24 (½-inch-thick) slices zucchini (about 4 medium)
1 fennel bulb, cut into 16 wedges
16 garlic cloves, peeled
½ teaspoon salt
¼ teaspoon black pepper
Cooking spray
Couscous (optional)

1. Combine first 7 ingredients in a zip-top plastic bag; seal and shake well. Marinate in refrigerator at least 1 hour. Remove chicken and vegetables from bag, and discard marinade.
2. Prepare grill.
3. Cook 16 garlic cloves in boiling water 3 minutes; drain and cool.
4. Thread 4 chicken cubes, 3 zucchini slices, 2 fennel wedges, and 2 garlic cloves alternately onto each of 8 (12-inch) skewers. Sprinkle with salt and pepper. Place kebabs on grill rack coated with cooking spray. Grill 8 minutes or until chicken is done, turning kebabs once. Serve with couscous, if desired. Yield: 4 servings (serving size: 2 kebabs).
Note: If using wooden skewers, soak them in water 30 minutes before grilling.

CALORIES 335 (34% from fat); FAT 12.6g (sat 2g, mono 8g, poly 1.6g); PROTEIN 41.8g; CARB 13.9g; FIBER 2.9g; CHOL 99mg; IRON 2.2mg; SODIUM 441mg; CALC 98mg

Serve these Mediterranean-inspired kebabs over couscous tossed with a bit of salt, cherry tomatoes, and chopped fresh mint.

Grilled Chicken Tostadas

Cilantro is the name for the leaf of the plant that is otherwise identified as coriander. Also known as Chinese parsley, the green leaves have a distinctive flavor and aroma generally described as citrusy, waxy, and soapy. Cilantro and coriander are an integral part of cuisines throughout the world, including Asian, Mexican, Indian, Tex-Mex, Caribbean, and North African foods. They are used in dishes ranging from fresh salsas to curries and soups. Wrap stems in damp paper towels, and store in the refrigerator wrapped in a plastic bag. Cilantro loses its flavor quickly, so rinse and chop just before you're ready to use it.

1½ pounds skinless, boneless chicken breast halves
1 tablespoon fresh lime juice
1 tablespoon 40%-less-sodium taco seasoning (such as Old El Paso)
½ teaspoon sugar
Cooking spray
6 (8-inch) flour tortillas
6 cups packaged coleslaw
1 (7-ounce) can green salsa
4 cups chopped tomato
¼ cup sliced ripe olives, chopped
1¼ cups fat-free refried beans
½ cup (2 ounces) crumbled feta cheese
6 tablespoons reduced-fat sour cream
¼ cup fresh cilantro leaves
¼ cup unsalted pumpkinseed kernels, toasted (optional)

1. Prepare grill, or heat a grill pan over medium-high heat.
2. Brush chicken with lime juice; sprinkle with taco seasoning and sugar. Place chicken on grill rack or grill pan coated with cooking spray; grill 4 minutes on each side or until done. Cool slightly. Cut chicken into ¼-inch strips; set aside. Place tortillas on grill rack or grill pan coated with cooking spray; grill 30 seconds on each side or until golden brown.
3. Combine coleslaw and salsa; toss to coat. Combine tomato and olives; toss gently.
4. Spread about 3 tablespoons beans over each tortilla; divide chicken evenly among tortillas. Top each serving with about ⅔ cup slaw mixture, ⅔ cup tomato mixture, 4 teaspoons cheese, 1 tablespoon sour cream, and 2 teaspoons cilantro. Sprinkle each serving with 2 teaspoons pumpkinseeds, if desired. Yield: 6 servings (serving size: 1 tostada).

CALORIES 361 (23% from fat); FAT 9.2g (sat 3.6g, mono 1.5g, poly 1.2g); PROTEIN 28.7g; CARB 43g; FIBER 6.8g; CHOL 65mg; IRON 3.7mg; SODIUM 844mg; CALC 221mg

Fried tortillas usually form the shells for tostadas, but grilling the tortillas lowers the fat. Prepared salsa, canned beans, and preshredded coleslaw make this recipe simple to prepare.

Greek Salad with Grilled Chicken

No need to spit out the seed anymore. This easy-to-use pitter is the perfect tool to handily remove olive and cherry pits. But the traditional method works well, too. Place olives on a cutting surface. Lay the wide, flat side of a heavy chef's knife on top, and give a good, sharp whack to the blade. The olives will pop open, exposing the pits for easy removal. To pit a large volume of olives, wrap them in a cloth towel, and smack them with a rolling pin or the bottom of a heavy skillet.

¼ cup fat-free, less-sodium chicken broth
2 tablespoons red wine vinegar
1 teaspoon sugar
1 teaspoon dried oregano
2 teaspoons olive oil
½ teaspoon salt
½ teaspoon freshly ground black pepper
1 garlic clove, minced
4 (6-ounce) skinless, boneless chicken breast halves
Cooking spray
8 cups torn romaine lettuce
1 cup sliced cucumber (about 1 small)
8 pitted kalamata olives, halved
4 plum tomatoes, quartered lengthwise
2 (¼-inch-thick) slices red onion, separated into rings
¼ cup (1 ounce) crumbled feta cheese

1. Prepare grill or preheat broiler.
2. Combine first 8 ingredients in a small bowl. Brush chicken with 2 tablespoons dressing, and set remaining dressing aside.
3. Place chicken on grill rack or broiler pan coated with cooking spray; cook 5 minutes on each side or until done. Cut into ¼-inch-thick slices.
4. Combine romaine lettuce and next 4 ingredients in a large bowl, and toss with remaining salad dressing. Divide salad evenly among 4 plates; top each serving with sliced chicken, and sprinkle with feta cheese. Yield: 4 servings (serving size: 2 cups salad, 3 ounces chicken, and 1 tablespoon feta cheese).

CALORIES 305 (27% from fat); FAT 9g (sat 2.6g, mono 4.2g, poly 1.3g); PROTEIN 43.3g; CARB 12.1g; FIBER 3.8g; CHOL 107mg; IRON 3.1mg; SODIUM 681mg; CALC 124mg

Prepare the zesty Greek dressing up to a week in advance; cover and store it in the refrigerator. Then let the dressing serve as both an enhancer for the grilled chicken and a dressing for the salad.

Grilled Chicken and Roasted Red Pepper Sandwiches with Fontina Cheese

Young fontina has a nutty, buttery flavor and a creamy texture. As it ages, the texture becomes drier, and the flavor mellows. It works well on a cheese tray and melts smoothly, making it great on these sandwiches, in quiche, or as a fondue.

1 pound skinless, boneless chicken breast halves
1 tablespoon fresh lemon juice
1 tablespoon Dijon mustard
2 teaspoons extravirgin olive oil
¼ teaspoon dried marjoram
¼ teaspoon dried thyme
1 garlic clove, minced and divided
Cooking spray
1 cup vertically sliced onion
1 teaspoon sugar
¾ teaspoon fennel seeds, crushed
¼ teaspoon crushed red pepper
¼ teaspoon salt
4 garlic cloves, minced
1 (7-ounce) bottle roasted red bell peppers, drained and sliced
1 tablespoon red wine vinegar
⅛ teaspoon freshly ground black pepper
1 (12-ounce) loaf rosemary focaccia, cut in half horizontally
4 teaspoons low-fat mayonnaise
3 ounces fontina cheese, thinly sliced

1. Place chicken between 2 sheets of heavy-duty plastic wrap, and pound to ¾-inch thickness using a meat mallet or rolling pin.
2. Combine lemon juice, next 5 ingredients, and chicken in a large zip-top plastic bag; seal. Marinate in refrigerator 2 hours, turning occasionally.
3. Heat a large nonstick skillet over medium-high heat. Coat pan with cooking spray. Add onion and next 5 ingredients; sauté 1 minute. Add roasted red bell peppers; cook 5 minutes or until onion is tender, stirring frequently. Stir in vinegar and black pepper.
4. Prepare grill.
5. Remove chicken from bag; discard marinade. Place chicken on grill rack coated with cooking spray; grill 5 minutes on each side or until done. Cool slightly; cut chicken into slices.
6. Spread cut sides of bread evenly with mayonnaise. Arrange cheese on bottom half of bread. Arrange chicken and bell pepper mixture over cheese. Top with top half of bread; press lightly.
7. Place stuffed loaf on grill rack; grill 3 minutes on each side or until cheese melts. Cut into quarters. Yield: 4 servings (serving size: 1 sandwich quarter).

CALORIES 462 (24% from fat); FAT 12.2g (sat 4.7g, mono 3.7g, poly 1.7g); PROTEIN 39.5g; CARB 51.2g; FIBER 5.6g; CHOL 90mg; IRON 3mg; SODIUM 981mg; CALC 199mg

For lunch or dinner, chicken sandwiches are always welcome at a casual-style meal. The sandwich grills just long enough for the cheese to melt over the chicken and spicy red pepper relish. Serve with vegetable chips or tomato soup.

Tandoori Chicken

Yogurt is a semisolid fermented milk product. Low-fat yogurt is a staple ingredient in the *Cooking Light* Test Kitchens, and it has a wide range of uses, from muffins to desserts. In Tandoori Chicken, diagonal cuts made across the chicken breasts allow the yogurt mixture to soak deeper into the meat. The natural acidity in the yogurt tenderizes the meat and adds tart flavor.

¾ cup coarsely chopped onion
1 teaspoon coarsely chopped peeled fresh ginger
2 garlic cloves, peeled
½ cup plain low-fat yogurt
1 tablespoon fresh lemon juice
1 teaspoon paprika
1 teaspoon ground cumin
1 teaspoon ground coriander seeds
½ teaspoon salt
½ teaspoon chili powder
¼ teaspoon black pepper
Dash of ground nutmeg
4 (6-ounce) skinless, boneless chicken breast halves
Cooking spray

1. Place first 3 ingredients in a food processor; process until finely chopped. Add yogurt and next 8 ingredients; pulse 4 times or until blended.
2. Make 3 (¼-inch-deep) diagonal cuts across top of each chicken breast half. Combine chicken and yogurt mixture in a large zip-top plastic bag. Seal and marinate in refrigerator 8 hours or overnight, turning occasionally.
3. Prepare grill or preheat broiler.
4. Remove chicken breast halves from bag; discard marinade. Place chicken on grill rack or broiler pan coated with cooking spray; cook 6 minutes on each side or until done. Yield: 4 servings (serving size: 1 chicken breast half).

CALORIES 208 (11% from fat); FAT 2.5g (sat 0.7g, mono 0.6g, poly 0.5g); PROTEIN 40.4g; CARB 3.5g; FIBER 0.5g; CHOL 100mg; IRON 1.5mg; SODIUM 272mg; CALC 55mg

Although it's not cooked in a tandoor oven, this entrée has all the flavors of the traditional Indian dish, thanks to a long marinating time. Serve with tabbouleh and pita chips.

Sesame-Chile Chicken with Gingered Watermelon Salsa

For ease of preparation, purchase a container of cut-up watermelon from the produce section of your supermarket; then all you'll have to do is cut the chunks into small pieces.

Chicken:
- 2 tablespoons low-sodium soy sauce
- 1 to 2 tablespoons chili sauce with garlic
- 1 tablespoon dark sesame oil
- 4 (6-ounce) skinless, boneless chicken breast halves

Salsa:
- 2 cups diced seeded watermelon
- ¼ cup diced yellow bell pepper
- 2 tablespoons thinly sliced green onions
- 1 tablespoon chopped fresh cilantro
- 2 teaspoons mirin (sweet rice wine)
- 1 teaspoon fresh lime juice
- 1 teaspoon grated peeled fresh ginger
- ⅛ teaspoon salt
- 1 jalapeño pepper, seeded and minced

Remaining Ingredients:
- ¼ teaspoon salt
- Cooking spray
- Hot cooked long-grain rice (optional)
- Cilantro sprigs (optional)
- Lime wedges (optional)

1. To prepare chicken, combine first 3 ingredients in a large zip-top plastic bag. Add chicken; seal and marinate in refrigerator 1 hour, turning occasionally.

2. Prepare grill.

3. To prepare salsa, combine watermelon and next 8 ingredients; cover and chill until ready to serve.

4. Remove chicken from marinade; discard marinade. Sprinkle chicken evenly with ¼ teaspoon salt. Place chicken on grill rack coated with cooking spray. Grill 6 minutes on each side or until done. Remove chicken from grill; let stand 5 minutes. Cut chicken diagonally across grain into thin slices; serve with salsa and over hot cooked rice, if desired. Garnish with cilantro sprigs and serve with lime wedges, if desired. Yield: 4 servings (serving size: 1 chicken breast half and about ½ cup salsa).

CALORIES 247 (17% from fat); FAT 4.6g (sat 0.9g, mono 1.5g, poly 1.5g); PROTEIN 40.2g; CARB 8.7g; FIBER 0.7g; CHOL 99mg; IRON 1.8mg; SODIUM 722mg; CALC 27mg

This dish delivers great taste and presentation, and it's easy to prepare, too. What more could you want? While the liquid from the salsa is tasty, you might want to use a slotted spoon to serve the salsa. Serve over a bed of jasmine or basmati rice.

Jerk-Style Chicken

A blender often works better than a food processor when you have a small volume of ingredients to process, such as for this marinade. Rather than pouring the mixture out of the container, it's easier to remove the bottom of the blender and use a rubber scraper to clean the sides and around the blades.

1 teaspoon grated lime rind
¼ cup fresh lime juice
2 tablespoons olive oil
1 to 2 tablespoons finely chopped jalapeño pepper
1 tablespoon ground allspice
1 tablespoon brown sugar
1 teaspoon salt
1 teaspoon coarsely ground black pepper
1 teaspoon dried thyme
1 teaspoon ground cinnamon
½ teaspoon ground nutmeg
3 garlic cloves
½ cup chopped onion
6 skinless, boneless chicken thighs (about 1⅛ pounds)
3 (6-ounce) skinless, boneless chicken breast halves
Cooking spray
Hot cooked long-grain rice (optional)
Parsley sprigs (optional)
Lime slices (optional)

1. Combine first 12 ingredients in a blender; process until well blended. Pour mixture into a large heavy-duty zip-top plastic bag; add onion and chicken. Seal bag; marinate in refrigerator 1 to 2 hours, turning bag occasionally.
2. Prepare grill.
3. Remove chicken from bag; discard marinade. Place chicken on grill rack coated with cooking spray. Grill chicken, covered, 5 minutes on each side or until done. Serve over hot cooked rice, and garnish with parsley and lime slices, if desired. Yield: 6 servings (serving size: 2 thighs or 1 breast half).

CALORIES 303 (37% from fat); FAT 12.6g (sat 3.2g, mono 5.5g, poly 2.6g); PROTEIN 41.9g; CARB 2.9g; FIBER 0.7g; CHOL 130mg; IRON 2mg; SODIUM 325mg; CALC 32mg

"Jerk" is a Jamaican cooking term used when chicken or pork is rubbed with a sweet-hot paste made from spices, herbs, and peppers and then cooked slowly over a fire of green pimiento wood. We achieved similar flavor results with the aid of a blender and grill.

Dry-Rub Chicken with Tangy Barbecue Sauce

Paprika is the dried, ground pods of *Capsicum annum*, a sweet red pepper. Most paprika is mild and slightly sweet in flavor. It also has a pleasantly fragrant aroma. The main thing to remember is that paprika only releases its flavor when heated. Thus, sprinkling ground paprika over colorless dishes may improve their appearance, but it does little for their taste. If you want to add overall color to a dish, stir the paprika into a little hot oil before adding. Kept in a cool, dark place, paprika retains its flavor for six to eight months. After that, it begins to lose its color and aroma, but it can still be used.

Chicken:
- 1 tablespoon paprika
- 2 teaspoons lemon pepper
- ½ teaspoon garlic powder
- ¼ teaspoon black pepper
- ⅛ teaspoon seasoned salt
- 3 bone-in chicken breast halves (about 1½ pounds), skinned
- 3 chicken drumsticks (about ¾ pound), skinned
- 3 bone-in chicken thighs (about 1 pound), skinned
- 2 cups water
- Cooking spray

Sauce:
- ½ cup ketchup
- ¼ cup fresh lemon juice
- 2 tablespoons cider vinegar
- 2 tablespoons honey
- ½ teaspoon garlic powder
- ¼ teaspoon black pepper

1. To prepare chicken, combine first 5 ingredients. Rub paprika mixture evenly over chicken pieces.

2. To prepare for indirect grilling on a charcoal grill, place a disposable aluminum foil pan in bottom of grill; pour 2 cups water in pan. Arrange charcoal around pan; prepare charcoal fire, and let burn 15 to 20 minutes. Coat grill rack with cooking spray; place rack on grill. Place chicken on grill rack over foil pan. Cover and grill 1½ hours or until a thermometer registers 180°. Remove chicken from grill; cover with foil, and let stand 5 minutes.

3. To prepare sauce, combine ketchup and next 5 ingredients in a small saucepan. Bring sauce to a simmer over medium-low heat; cook 15 minutes, stirring frequently. Serve sauce with chicken. Yield: 6 servings (serving size: 4 teaspoons sauce, 1 breast half or 1 thigh and 1 drumstick).

Note: To prepare for indirect grilling on a gas grill, preheat grill to medium-hot using both burners. After preheating, turn left burner off (leave right burner on). Place a disposable foil pan on briquettes on left side. Pour 2 cups water in pan. Coat grill rack with cooking spray; place rack on grill. Place chicken on grill rack covering left burner, and proceed with method as directed above.

CALORIES 221 (17% from fat); FAT 4.1g (sat 1g, mono 1.2g, poly 1.1g); PROTEIN 32.7g; CARB 13.2g; FIBER 0.7g; CHOL 104mg; IRON 1.8mg; SODIUM 405mg; CALC 24mg

A dry rub is a mixture of ground spices and herbs that's rubbed or pressed onto the surface of poultry or meat before it's grilled or baked. Many recipes suggest that food should marinate in the refrigerator several hours to absorb the flavor of the rub. However, we found that slow indirect grilling allowed enough time for this rub to flavor the chicken. The smokiness of the paprika in this rub complements the sweetness of the sauce very well. It may even inspire you to create your own rub.

casual entertaining

Honey-Ginger Chicken Bites

Look for fresh ginger in the produce section of your supermarket. Choose the freshest, youngest-looking ginger you can find. Old ginger is fibrous, tough, and flavorless. Use a vegetable peeler or paring knife to remove the tough skin and reveal the yellowish flesh. Like garlic, you can mince ginger with a sharp knife, or you can use a garlic press.

⅔ cup honey
2 tablespoons minced peeled fresh ginger
2 tablespoons fresh lemon juice
2 tablespoons cider vinegar
2 tablespoons low-sodium soy sauce
2 teaspoons dark sesame oil
1 teaspoon grated orange rind
1 teaspoon Worcestershire sauce
4 garlic cloves, minced
1¼ pounds skinless, boneless chicken thighs, cut into bite-sized pieces (about 16 pieces)
Cooking spray
1 teaspoon salt
¼ teaspoon black pepper
2 teaspoons cornstarch
2 teaspoons water
2 teaspoons sesame seeds, toasted (optional)

1. Combine first 9 ingredients in a large zip-top plastic bag; seal and shake well. Add chicken; seal and toss to coat. Refrigerate at least 2 hours or overnight, turning occasionally.

2. Preheat oven to 425°.

3. Remove chicken from bag, reserving marinade. Arrange chicken in a single layer on the rack of a broiler pan coated with cooking spray. Sprinkle chicken with salt and pepper. Bake at 425° for 20 minutes, stirring once.

4. While chicken is cooking, strain marinade through a sieve into a bowl; discard solids. Place marinade in a saucepan; bring to a boil. Cook 3 minutes; skim solids from surface. Combine cornstarch and water in a small bowl; stir with a whisk. Add cornstarch mixture to pan, stirring with a whisk; cook 1 minute. Remove from heat; pour glaze into a large bowl.

5. Preheat broiler.

6. Add chicken to glaze; toss well to coat. Place chicken mixture on a jelly-roll pan; broil 5 minutes or until browned, stirring twice. Sprinkle with sesame seeds, if desired. Yield: 12 servings (serving size: about 1½ ounces).

CALORIES 179 (22% from fat); FAT: 4.4g (sat 1g, mono 1.4g, poly 1.2g); PROTEIN 18.2g; CARB 18.2g; FIBER 0.1g; CHOL 76mg; IRON: 1.1mg; SODIUM 430mg; CALC 14mg

These bite-sized appetizers are steeped in a mixture of garlic, soy sauce, ginger, citrus, and honey. The marinade is then reduced and used to glaze the chicken. These are perfect for any gathering—from a Super Bowl gathering to an Oscar party.

Raspberry-Balsamic Glazed Chicken

1 teaspoon vegetable oil
Cooking spray
½ cup chopped red onion
1½ teaspoons minced fresh or
  ½ teaspoon dried thyme
½ teaspoon salt, divided
4 (6-ounce) skinless, boneless
  chicken breast halves
⅓ cup seedless raspberry
  preserves
2 tablespoons balsamic
  vinegar
¼ teaspoon black pepper

1. Heat oil in a large nonstick skillet coated with cooking spray over medium-high heat. Add onion; sauté 5 minutes. Combine thyme and ¼ teaspoon salt; sprinkle over chicken. Add chicken to pan; sauté 6 minutes on each side or until done. Remove chicken from pan; keep warm.
2. Reduce heat to medium-low. Add remaining ¼ teaspoon salt, preserves, vinegar, and pepper, stirring constantly until preserves melt. Spoon raspberry sauce over chicken. Yield: 4 servings (serving size: 1 chicken breast half and 2 tablespoons sauce).

CALORIES 277 (11% from fat); FAT 3.3g (sat 0.7g, mono 1g, poly 1g); PROTEIN 39.5g; CARB 20.6g; FIBER 0.3g; CHOL 99mg; IRON 1.4mg; SODIUM 113mg; CALC 27mg

Consider moving your jams, jellies, and preserves from the breakfast table to the dinner table. The fruit flavors are already concentrated, so use this to your advantage. Combine a couple of tablespoons of your favorite flavor with a splash of balsamic or red wine vinegar, chicken broth, wine, or even a little water. Use this mixture to deglaze the skillet. It's the perfect way to add rich flavor to sautéed chicken breasts.

This is your "go-to" recipe when time is short and your guests are about to arrive. While this tasty, quick-and-easy dish is perfect as is, consider substituting other varieties of fruit preserves, such as apricot, blackberry, or peach. Pair it with brown rice and vegetables, and you have a great meal!

Chicken with Lemon-Caper Sauce

¼ teaspoon salt, divided
¼ teaspoon black pepper, divided
4 (6-ounce) skinless, boneless chicken breast halves
1 tablespoon olive oil
Cooking spray
⅓ cup extradry vermouth
3 tablespoons fresh lemon juice
1½ tablespoons capers
1 tablespoon chopped fresh parsley
Hot cooked spaghetti (optional)

1. Sprinkle ⅛ teaspoon salt and ⅛ teaspoon pepper over chicken. Heat oil in a large nonstick skillet coated with cooking spray over medium-high heat. Add chicken; cook 6 minutes on each side or until done. Remove from pan. Set aside; keep warm.

2. Add remaining ⅛ teaspoon salt, remaining ⅛ teaspoon pepper, vermouth, lemon juice, and capers to pan, scraping pan to loosen browned bits. Cook until reduced to ¼ cup (about 2 minutes). Stir in chopped parsley. Spoon sauce over chicken. Serve over spaghetti, if desired. Yield: 4 servings (serving size: 1 chicken breast half and 1 tablespoon sauce).

CALORIES 222 (22% from fat); FAT 5.5g (sat 1g, mono 3g, poly 0.8g); PROTEIN 39.6g; CARB 1.5g; FIBER 0.1g; CHOL 99mg; IRON 1.5mg; SODIUM 377mg; CALC 25mg

You can find capers in the condiment section of your supermarket. The smaller immature buds are more expensive, but they're also the most intensely flavored. Larger capers (from raisin-size to the size of a small olive) are fine to use, too. At any size, capers have an assertive flavor, and you will find that even a somewhat pricey bottle will last up to a year in the refrigerator.

Measure ingredients for this recipe ahead, and then enjoy a glass of wine with company before the meal. You can have this dinner on the table in 15 to 20 minutes. It'll be so yummy that your guests will clean their plates. You may want to consider doubling the sauce to serve over noodles or rice.

Chicken Parmesan

Dredging the chicken breasts in flour is what gives them a nice brown exterior when cooked. The wetness of the chicken and the egg bath helps the flour to adhere to the chicken breasts. Organize your work space so that you can use one hand for dipping the breasts in the egg white and the other hand for dredging the chicken in flour.

Tomato Sauce:
- 1 ounce sun-dried tomatoes, packed without oil (about ¼ cup)
- 1 cup boiling water
- 1 teaspoon olive oil
- 2 cups chopped red bell pepper
- 1 cup chopped onion
- 2 (14.5-ounce) cans diced tomatoes, undrained
- ¼ cup chopped fresh parsley
- 2 tablespoons chopped fresh basil
- 1 tablespoon balsamic vinegar
- ¼ teaspoon black pepper
- 2 garlic cloves, minced

Chicken:
- ¼ cup all-purpose flour
- ¼ cup grated Parmesan cheese
- ¼ teaspoon black pepper
- 4 (6-ounce) skinless, boneless chicken breast halves
- 1 large egg white, lightly beaten
- 1 tablespoon olive oil
- Cooking spray
- 1 cup (4 ounces) shredded part-skim mozzarella cheese
- 3 cups hot cooked linguine (about 6 ounces uncooked pasta)

1. To prepare tomato sauce, combine sun-dried tomatoes and water in a bowl; cover and let stand 30 minutes or until soft. Drain and finely chop tomatoes.

2. Heat 1 teaspoon olive oil in a large saucepan over medium-high heat. Add sun-dried tomatoes, bell pepper, and onion; sauté 7 minutes. Stir in canned tomatoes; bring to a boil. Cover, reduce heat, and simmer 10 minutes. Remove from heat; stir in parsley, basil, vinegar, ¼ teaspoon black pepper, and garlic.

3. Preheat oven to 350°.

4. To prepare chicken, lightly spoon flour into a dry measuring cup; level with a knife. Combine flour, Parmesan, and ¼ teaspoon black pepper in a shallow dish. Place each chicken breast half between 2 sheets of heavy-duty plastic wrap; pound to ¼-inch thickness using a meat mallet or rolling pin. Dip each breast half in egg white; dredge in flour mixture.

5. Heat 1 tablespoon oil in a large nonstick skillet over medium-high heat. Add chicken, and cook 5 minutes on each side or until golden. Arrange in a 13 x 9–inch baking dish coated with cooking spray. Pour tomato sauce over chicken. Sprinkle with mozzarella. Bake at 350° for 15 minutes or until chicken is done. Serve over linguine. Yield: 4 servings (serving size: 1 chicken breast half, 1 cup sauce, ¼ cup cheese, and ¾ cup pasta).

CALORIES 593 (21% from fat); FAT 13.6g (sat 5.1g, mono 5.6g, poly 1.3g); PROTEIN 58.8g; CARB 58.7g; FIBER 7g; CHOL 119mg; IRON 4.7mg; SODIUM 672mg; CALC 327mg

This chicken is very tasty, not to mention crispy on the outside and juicy on the inside. If you're short on time, add chopped fresh parsley and basil to your favorite bottled pasta sauce, and continue with the recipe beginning with step three.

Chicken Marsala

Clarified butter (butter without the milk solids) is ideal for searing meats because it can be heated to a high temperature without burning. Although you can purchase clarified butter, we detail how to make it in the first step of the recipe for Chicken Marsala. Clarified butter can be prepared, chilled, and reheated when ready for use, or it can be frozen up to two months.

4 tablespoons butter, divided
Cooking spray
1 (8-ounce) package presliced mushrooms
2 tablespoons finely chopped shallots
1 tablespoon minced fresh garlic
4 (6-ounce) skinless, boneless chicken breast halves
¼ teaspoon salt, divided
¼ teaspoon black pepper, divided
3 tablespoons all-purpose flour
¾ cup fat-free, less-sodium chicken broth
½ cup dry Marsala wine
½ cup frozen green peas
2 tablespoons half-and-half
4 cups hot cooked fettuccine (about 8 ounces uncooked pasta)

1. Place 3 tablespoons butter in a small glass measuring cup. Microwave at MEDIUM-HIGH 45 seconds or until butter melts. Let stand 1 minute. Skim foam from surface; discard. Pour melted butter through a fine sieve over a small bowl; discard milk solids. Set clarified butter aside.
2. Heat a large nonstick skillet over medium-high heat. Coat pan with cooking spray. Add mushrooms, shallots, and garlic. Cook 3 minutes or until moisture evaporates; remove mushroom mixture from pan. Set aside.
3. Place each chicken breast half between 2 sheets of heavy-duty plastic wrap, and pound to ¼-inch thickness using a meat mallet or rolling pin. Sprinkle both sides of chicken with ⅛ teaspoon salt and ⅛ teaspoon pepper. Place flour in a shallow dish; dredge chicken breast halves in flour.
4. Add clarified butter to pan, and place over medium-high heat. Add chicken; cook 3 minutes on each side or until lightly browned. Remove chicken from pan. Return mushroom mixture to pan; add broth and Marsala, scraping pan to loosen browned bits. Bring mixture to a boil, reduce heat, and simmer 5 minutes or until reduced to 1 cup. Stir in peas; cook 1 minute. Add remaining 1 tablespoon butter, remaining ⅛ teaspoon salt, remaining ⅛ teaspoon pepper, and half-and-half, stirring until butter melts. Return chicken to pan, and cook until thoroughly heated and chicken is done. Serve chicken and sauce over pasta. Yield: 4 servings (serving size: 1 chicken breast half, 1 cup pasta, and ¼ cup sauce).

CALORIES 585 (24% from fat); FAT 15.3g (sat 8.4g, mono 4.1g, poly 1g); PROTEIN 51.4g; CARB 55g; FIBER 3.7g; CHOL 133mg; IRON 4.4mg; SODIUM 469mg; CALC 57mg

Marsala, an Italian fortified wine, adds a touch of smoky flavor to the sauce. Put the pasta water on to boil as you begin the recipe so the fettuccine can cook at the same time as the chicken.

Breast of Chicken Oaxaca

To cut a pocket in a chicken breast, start by placing the chicken breast half on a cutting board, and trim all visible fat from chicken. Then insert tip of a thin, sharp knife (such as a boning knife) into thickest side of the chicken breast. Make a 2-inch slit. Cut to, but not through, the opposite side of the breast.

Chipotle Sauce:

- ¼ cup hot water
- ½ teaspoon chicken-flavored bouillon granules
- 4 canned chipotle chiles in adobo sauce
- ¾ cup reduced-fat sour cream
- 1 tablespoon lime juice

Chicken:

- 1 peeled avocado, cut into 6 wedges
- 1 tablespoon lime juice
- 6 (6-ounce) skinless, boneless chicken breast halves
- ¾ cup (3 ounces) shredded asadero or Monterey Jack cheese
- ¼ teaspoon salt
- ⅛ teaspoon white pepper
- 2 tablespoons all-purpose flour
- 3 large egg whites, lightly beaten
- 1 cup seasoned breadcrumbs
- 1 tablespoon vegetable oil
- Cooking spray

Remaining Ingredients:

- 8 cups hot cooked linguine (about 1 pound uncooked pasta)
- ¼ cup sliced ripe olives
- 2 tablespoons cilantro

1. To prepare chipotle sauce, combine first 3 ingredients in a blender; process until smooth. Pour sauce into a bowl; stir in sour cream and 1 tablespoon lime juice.

2. To prepare chicken, toss avocado with 1 tablespoon lime juice. Cut a horizontal slit through thickest portion of each breast half to form a pocket. Stuff 1 avocado slice and 2 tablespoons cheese into each pocket. Sprinkle chicken with salt and pepper, and dredge chicken in flour. Dip chicken in egg whites; dredge in breadcrumbs.

3. Heat oil in a large nonstick skillet coated with cooking spray over medium-high heat. Add chicken; sauté 6 to 7 minutes on each side or until done.

4. Toss pasta with olives and cilantro. Place 1⅓ cups pasta on each of 6 plates. Top each serving with 1 chicken breast and about 3 tablespoons chipotle sauce. Yield: 6 servings.

CALORIES 702 (24% from fat); FAT 18.5g (sat 7.1g, mono 5.5g, poly 2.4g); PROTEIN 54.4g; CARB 77.8g; FIBER 5.4g; CHOL 125mg; IRON 5.4mg; SODIUM 919mg; CALC 220mg

This decadent dish is from the restaurant Casa del Sol in Ciudad Juárez, Mexico, just across the border from El Paso. Asadero cheese, also called Oaxaca or Chihuahua cheese, is a good melting cheese similar to Monterey Jack and is how this recipe gets its name. We sautéed the chicken breasts in a small amount of oil instead of frying them, and we used reduced-fat sour cream in the chipotle sauce in place of heavy cream.

Chicken in Wine Cream Sauce

Rice and wild rice are not the same thing. In fact, wild rice isn't rice at all—it's the seed of an annual water grass, *Zizania aquatica*, which is natural to the cold waters of Minnesota and Canada. Wild rice serves as a perfect accent to both savory and sweet ingredients. However you decide to use it, remember its untamed origins—a little wild rice goes a long way, and even a modest amount can make a dramatic difference in a meal.

2 teaspoons dried oregano
2 teaspoons dried basil
1½ teaspoons dried rosemary
1 teaspoon garlic powder
½ teaspoon salt
½ teaspoon black pepper
¼ teaspoon paprika
1 tablespoon plus 1 teaspoon olive oil, divided
8 bone-in chicken thighs, skinned
Cooking spray
⅓ cup all-purpose flour
2¼ cups 1% low-fat milk
1 cup dry white wine
2 cups sliced mushrooms
¼ cup tub-style light cream cheese
2 cups hot cooked wild rice
Oregano sprigs (optional)

1. Combine first 7 ingredients and 2 teaspoons olive oil in a small bowl; rub over chicken. Heat remaining 2 teaspoons oil in a large skillet coated with cooking spray over medium-high heat. Add chicken; cook 5 minutes on each side or until browned. Remove chicken from pan, and set aside.

2. Lightly spoon flour into a dry measuring cup; level with a knife. Place flour in a bowl; gradually add milk and wine, stirring with a whisk until blended. Add mixture to pan, scraping pan to loosen browned bits; bring to a simmer. Return chicken to pan; cover, reduce heat, and simmer 30 minutes or until chicken is done. Add mushrooms; cover and simmer 5 minutes. Remove chicken from pan; cover and set aside.

3. Add cheese to pan; cook, stirring constantly with a whisk, 5 minutes or until cheese melts. Place ½ cup rice on each of 4 plates. Top each with 2 chicken thighs and 1 cup sauce. Garnish with oregano sprigs, if desired. Yield: 4 servings.

CALORIES 444 (29% from fat); FAT 14.5g (sat 4.4g, mono 6.2g, poly 2.2g); PROTEIN 39.1g; CARB 39g; FIBER 2.5g; CHOL 128mg; IRON 4mg; SODIUM 568mg; CALC 246mg

If you wish to impress guests, Chicken in Wine Cream Sauce is the way to go. It's just like something you'd find in a fancy restaurant—only it's easy to make and adaptable to whatever ingredients you have on hand, such as brown rice or a commercial wild rice blend.

Chicken and Leeks Braised in Wine

Dirt is sometimes trapped between the layers of leeks. To clean, cut the root end, and then slit the leek lengthwise. Fan out the layers, and rinse under cold water.

Cooking spray
8 bone-in chicken thighs, skinned (about 2 pounds)
¾ teaspoon salt, divided
½ teaspoon freshly ground black pepper, divided
4 leeks (about 2¼ pounds), cut diagonally into 2-inch pieces
1 teaspoon ground coriander
1 (3-inch) cinnamon stick
2 cups riesling or other slightly sweet white wine
1 teaspoon sugar
2 bay leaves
2 oregano sprigs
2 garlic cloves, peeled
1 (5 x 1–inch) orange rind strip
3 cups chopped seeded peeled tomato
1 tablespoon chopped fresh oregano
Parsley sprigs (optional)

1. Heat a large nonstick skillet over medium-high heat. Coat pan with cooking spray. Sprinkle chicken with ½ teaspoon salt and ¼ teaspoon pepper. Add chicken to pan; sauté 4 minutes on each side. Remove from pan. Add leeks to pan; sauté 4 minutes or until browned, turning once. Remove from pan.

2. Add coriander and cinnamon to pan; cook 30 seconds. Add wine and next 5 ingredients, and bring to a boil. Cover, reduce heat, and simmer 3 minutes. Add leeks. Cover and cook 5 minutes. Add chicken. Cover and cook 8 minutes.

3. Add tomato; bring to a boil. Reduce heat, and cook, uncovered, 10 minutes or until chicken is done, stirring frequently. Remove cinnamon stick, bay leaves, and rind.

4. Stir in remaining ¼ teaspoon salt, remaining ¼ teaspoon pepper, and chopped oregano. Garnish each serving with parsley sprigs, if desired. Yield: 4 servings (serving size: 2 thighs, about 2 leek pieces, and ½ cup sauce).

CALORIES 357 (17% from fat); FAT 6.6g (sat 1.5g, mono 1.8g, poly 1.9g); PROTEIN 30.9g; CARB 46.7g; FIBER 6.8g; CHOL 107mg; IRON 8.2mg; SODIUM 624mg; CALC 199mg

Once cut diagonally into 2-inch pieces, the leeks soften and develop a delicate flavor but remain intact for a nice presentation. Complete the meal with a salad of crisp lettuce, cucumber, tomato, and feta topped with a lemon-mint dressing.

Chicken with 40 Cloves of Garlic

2½ cups chopped onion
1 teaspoon dried tarragon
6 parsley sprigs
4 celery stalks, each cut into
  3 pieces
8 bone-in chicken thighs,
  skinned (about 2¾ pounds)
8 chicken drumsticks, skinned
  (about 2 pounds)
½ cup dry vermouth or white
  wine
1½ teaspoons salt
¼ teaspoon black pepper
Dash of ground nutmeg
40 garlic cloves, unpeeled
  (about 4 heads)
Tarragon sprigs (optional)
French bread (optional)

1. Preheat oven to 375°.
2. Combine first 4 ingredients in a 4-quart casserole. Arrange chicken pieces over vegetable and herb mixture. Drizzle with vermouth, and sprinkle with salt, pepper, and nutmeg. Nestle garlic around chicken. Cover casserole with foil and casserole lid.
3. Bake at 375° for 1½ hours or until chicken is done. Garnish with tarragon sprigs, and serve with French bread, if desired. Yield: 8 servings (serving size: 1 thigh, 1 drumstick, ¼ cup vegetable and herb mixture, and 5 garlic cloves).

CALORIES 277 (34% from fat); FAT 10.4g (sat 2.8g, mono 3.8g, poly 2.4g); PROTEIN 33.1g; CARB 11.7g; FIBER 1.6g; CHOL 110mg; IRON 2.2mg; SODIUM 573mg; CALC 67mg

Garlic is a powerfully flavored member of the onion family, and it's an indispensable ingredient in many cuisines and dishes. Garlic is grown in bulbs, which are made up of sections called cloves. Each garlic clove is encased in its own parchmentlike skin. Roasting whole garlic cloves in the skin mellows the flavor, while chopping intensifies the taste.

Don't let the amount of garlic in this dish scare you away. The garlic flavor mellows as it cooks alongside the chicken. And the garlic is meant to be eaten, too. Simply squeeze the cloves between your fingers to discover a delectable garlic paste that's perfect for spreading on warm bread.

all about
Chicken

In this Cooking Class, you'll find answers to the most frequently asked questions about chicken, along with must-have information on chicken selection, safety, and preparation techniques for cooking delicious chicken every time.

Purchasing Chicken

The recipe ingredient list is your guide in selecting the best type of chicken (fresh, frozen, or precooked) for each recipe.

Fresh Whole Chicken

• *Broiler-fryers* weigh 3 to 4 pounds. While they are very tender and juicy when roasted or baked, they don't have as much meat as roasters. They are best used for recipes that call for cut-up fryers or for making chicken stock.

• *Roasters* weigh 4 to 7 pounds. If you want to roast or bake a whole chicken, think big. Large roasters have wonderful flavor and a greater proportion of meat to bone, and any leftovers are a time-saver.

• *Stewing hens* are tough old birds, best used for chicken and dumplings or

soup. When roasted, the meat becomes even tougher. However, when simmered slowly in plenty of liquid, the meat becomes fall-off-the-bone tender, and the remaining broth is wonderfully rich and flavorful.

Organic and Free-Range Chicken

We tasted both organic chicken and free-range chicken side by side with conventionally farmed chicken to see if we could tell a difference in the flavor and tenderness. What we found was that both organic and free-range chickens have a "cleaner" chicken flavor and a better texture than conventionally farmed chicken. But are they worth the extra expense? Unless you're cooking simple roasted chicken, probably not.

Fresh Chicken Pieces

Fresh chicken comes packaged in many ways. Read the labels carefully to check for specific pieces, size and weight, and for added flavor enhancers.

• *Chicken breasts (skinless, bone-in or boneless)* are a staple of healthful cooking because they are lean and versatile, and they cook in a flash. The size of chicken breasts can vary greatly, even within the same package, but plan on 6-ounces of uncooked meat per serving. Look for 6-ounce skinless, boneless chicken breast halves or 8-ounce skinless, bone-in chicken breast halves.

Some brands of chicken breasts now on the market are injected with a sodium broth for added juiciness. If the chicken has been injected, a statement will be on the label. While some brands of injected chicken seem moister than noninjected breasts after cooking, they can also taste a little too salty. We tend to use the noninjected chicken breasts most often.

• *Chicken tenders*, while more expensive than chicken breasts, save prep and cook time. They are good for recipes that call for long, thin strips of meat. The size of chicken tenders will vary, so buy an amount that equals 6 ounces per serving. As a substitute, cut boneless chicken breasts into strips.

• *Chicken thighs (skinless, bone-in or boneless)* rule when it comes to flavor, and they're significantly less expensive than chicken breasts. Chicken thighs are a good choice for long-simmering, robustly flavored dishes. The size of thighs can vary, but plan on about 6 ounces of uncooked meat per serving. Usually one serving is two 4-ounce bone-in thighs, skinned, or two 3-ounce skinless, boneless thighs. If your fresh-meat counter doesn't carry boneless, skinless thighs, you can debone your own.

Frozen Chicken

Individually frozen portions of bone-in and boneless chicken breast halves, tenders, thighs, and drumsticks are readily available in the supermarket. The chicken pieces are marinated to enhance juiciness and tenderness. Because they are marinated, these frozen chicken pieces are higher in sodium than their fresh, noninjected

counterparts. They are frozen individually and packed loosely in resealable bags. Remove what you need for a given recipe, and keep the remainder frozen.

Precooked Chicken

If your recipe calls for cooked chicken and you don't have any leftovers to use, you have several options.

• *Poached chicken breasts*. Keep skinless, boneless chicken breasts on hand, and you can have cooked chicken ready for your recipe in about 20 minutes.

For a yield of about 3 cups chopped, cooked chicken, place 3 (6-ounce) skinless, boneless chicken breasts in a large skillet, and add about 1½ cups water. Bring to a boil. Cover, reduce heat, and simmer 14 minutes or until chicken is no longer pink. Drain. Slice, chop, or shred chicken as directed in the recipe. If the recipe calls for cold chicken, cover the cooked chicken, and refrigerate for at least two hours. Or freeze for 30 minutes or until thoroughly chilled.

• *Refrigerated or frozen cooked chicken*. Look for packages of chopped cooked chicken in the frozen-foods section of your supermarket. Single servings of roasted chicken breasts or drumsticks, grilled chicken strips, and whole roasted chickens can be found in the meat department. Refrigerated or frozen cooked chicken is higher in sodium than chicken that you cook yourself.

• *Store-cooked chicken*. Deli-roasted or rotisserie chicken from the supermarket

is our favorite option when a recipe calls for cooked chicken. A rotisserie chicken keeps for three to four days in the refrigerator and is great to keep on hand for a quick meal. It's easy to slice and to remove the meat from the bone. If you're adding rotisserie chicken to a hot recipe, stir it in at the end to warm it up. You can choose from a variety of flavors, from plain to barbecue to herb-roasted. Most of the seasoning (and the salt) is in the skin; once the skin is removed, these chickens are comparable to fresh-cooked chicken in terms of fat, and they're only slightly higher in sodium. When buying rotisserie chicken at the grocery store, pick it up at the end of your shopping trip so it stays hot until you get home. Serve or refrigerate it within two hours, or sooner in hot weather.

Precooked Chicken Substitutions

If you're using precooked chicken in a recipe, here are some useful substitution amounts:

Type	Cup Measures
1 pound uncooked skinless, boneless chicken	3 cups chopped cooked chicken
1 (6-ounce) skinless, boneless chicken breast	1 cup chopped cooked chicken
1 (2-pound) uncooked chicken	2¼ cups chopped cooked chicken
1 (2-pound) rotisserie chicken	3–3½ cups chopped cooked chicken
1 (6-ounce) package grilled chicken strips	1⅓ cups chopped cooked chicken
1 (9-ounce) package frozen chopped cooked chicken	1⅔ cups chopped cooked chicken

How Much Chicken to Buy

We call for 6-ounce portions (excluding skin and bones) of uncooked chicken per serving in our recipes.

Type	Number of Pieces and/or Weight	Number of Servings
Broiler-fryer	1 (3–4 pounds)	4
Whole roaster	1 (6–7 pounds)	8
Skinless, boneless chicken breast	1 (6-ounce)	1
Skinless, bone-in chicken breast	1 (8-ounce)	1
Chicken tenders	6 ounces (number may vary)	1
Skinless, boneless chicken thighs	2 (3 ounce)	1
Skinless, bone-in chicken thighs	2 (4-ounce)	1
Drumsticks	2 (4-ounce)	1

Chicken Safety

Chicken is highly perishable and should be handled carefully to prevent foodborne illness. Check the "sell by" date on the package label before purchasing. This shows the last day the product should be sold.

Storing Refrigerate raw chicken up to two days and cooked chicken up to three days. Raw skinless, boneless chicken can marinate in the refrigerator up to eight hours; raw chicken pieces with skin and bone can marinate for up to one day. Freeze uncooked chicken up to six months and cooked chicken up to three months.

Thawing You can thaw frozen chicken in the refrigerator or in cold water. Allow about five hours per pound of frozen chicken to thaw in the refrigerator. For the cold-water method, submerge the chicken—still in its wrapping—in a sink or pot of cold water, and change the water every 30 minutes until it's thawed.

Handling Wash your hands well with hot water and plenty of soap before and after handling chicken. Use hot water and soap to wash the cutting board and any utensils that come in contact with the chicken. When you rinse chicken, be careful that you don't splash water from the chicken onto countertops where unwrapped foods such as fruit, vegetables, or salad greens may be.

Cooking To prevent foodborne illnesses, chicken must be cooked to the correct temperature:

- Whole chicken   180°
- Chicken legs and thighs 180°
- Chicken breasts   170°

For whole chicken, use an instant-read thermometer inserted into the thickest part of the thigh to confirm the temperature. For breasts, legs, and thighs, pierce with a fork—the juices will run clear when the chicken is done. For more guidance on poultry, call the USDA Meat and Poultry Hotline (888-MPHotline or 888-674-6854).

Essential Techniques for Perfectly Cooked Chicken

Use these cooking tips and techniques as a quick reference when cooking chicken.

To achieve perfectly cooked chicken, you should begin by removing the skin. Removing the skin reduces the fat grams by about half. And for this very reason, *Cooking Light* usually calls for skinless breasts and thighs. However, for roasted whole chickens, we usually leave the skin on because it protects the meat from drying out. For recipes that call for roasted whole chicken, rub herbs and spices under the skin before cooking, and then remove the skin before serving. The fat savings will still be substantial, and the lingering herbs and spices will still cling to the meat.

1. Before cooking chicken, remove the skin and fat with kitchen shears. You'll discover that kitchen shears will work better than a knife. Removing the skin will reduce the fat grams by about half.

2. Place the chicken between two sheets of plastic wrap. Pound chicken to ¼- to ½-inch thickness using a meat mallet or a rolling pin.

3. Pierce each chicken breast with a fork to tell if the chicken is cooked completely. If the juices run clear, it is done.

4. Add liquid such as broth, wine, vinegar, or water to the skillet after you've cooked the chicken, and scrape the bottom to loosen the browned bits.

5. A general rule is to cook the sauce until about half of it remains. After cooking, pour the sauce into a measuring cup to be sure that it has reduced.

How to make a pocket in a chicken breast:

1. Place the chicken breast half on a cutting board; trim all visible fat. Insert the tip of a thin, sharp knife (such as a boning knife) into the thickest side of the chicken breast. Make a 2-inch slit.

2. Using your fingers, stuff the breast, getting as much filling as you can into the pocket.

How to debone a chicken thigh:

1. Place the chicken thigh on a cutting board; trim all visible fat with kitchen shears. Work from the inside of the thigh, and cut along both sides of the thigh bone, separating the bone from the meat.

2. Cut around the cartilage at the joint, and remove the thigh bone and cartilage.

Chicken Accompaniments

Side dishes are to chicken what butter is to bread. Without them, there's just something missing from the meal. If the side dish isn't included in a recipe, we often give "serve with" suggestions. Some of our favorites are listed below. But you don't have to be tied to these suggestions. Instead, mix and match flavors and textures to create your own mouth-watering meals.

• Grilled or roasted vegetables such as asparagus, corn on the cob, green beans, and tomatoes
• Steamed or sautéed vegetables such as broccoli, spinach, and zucchini
• Mixed green salads
• Baked and mashed potatoes and sweet potatoes
• Roasted potato wedges
• Brown, white, jasmine, basmati, or wild rice
• Couscous or polenta
• Pasta such as orzo, fettuccine, linguine, or spaghetti

Subject Index

Recipe Index

143